UNDERSTANDING
PHILOSOPHY

ANCIENT AND
HELLENISTIC THOUGHT

UNDERSTANDING PHILOSOPHY

Ancient and Hellenistic Thought

Medieval and Modern Philosophy

Contemporary Thought

UNDERSTANDING
PHILOSOPHY

ANCIENT AND
HELLENISTIC THOUGHT

JOAN A. PRICE

CHELSEA HOUSE
PUBLISHERS
An imprint of Infobase Publishing

To Ann, A Plato in the making.

《⊙ ⊙》

Ancient and Hellenistic Thought

Copyright © 2008 by Infobase Publishing

Chelsea House
An imprint of Infobase Publishing
132 West 31st Street
New York NY 10001

Library of Congress Cataloging-in-Publication Data

Price, Joan A.
  Ancient and Hellenistic thought / Joan Price.
    p. cm. — (Understanding philosophy)
  Includes bibliographical references and index.
  ISBN 978-0-7910-8739-8 (hardcover)
  1. Philosophy, Ancient. I. Title. II. Series.

  B111.P75 2007
  180—dc22   2007028320

Series design by Erika K. Arroyo
Cover design by Ben Peterson

Printed in the United States of America

Bang FOF 10 9 8 7 6 5 4 3

This book is printed on acid-free paper.

All links and Web addresses were checked and verified to be correct at the time of the Web, some addresses and ꞁay no longer be valid.

CONTENTS

1

THE PRE-SOCRATICS: EARLY GREEK PHILOSOPHERS

Philosophy has its origin in our sense of wonder.
—Aristotle

The earliest philosophers in the Western world were the pre-Socratic philosophers, or those who lived before Socrates (469–399 B.C.). These pioneering thinkers offer us insight into the first philosophical questions asked and the first answers given about the nature of the world and we who live in it.

In about 600 B.C., these philosophers asked questions such as, "How did the world come into being?" and, "What is the world made of?" They wanted to know what holds everything together so that Earth and everything in it does not fly apart.

BEFORE THE PRE-SOCRATICS

Before 600 B.C., people found answers to all of their questions about life and the world in which they lived in various religious myths handed down from generation to generation by word of mouth. Often, gods or superhuman beings served as the explanation. Greeks saw gods and superhuman beings as the ones who held power over nature and humans. Today, we take for granted that we can forecast weather. We know what causes rain, floods, and droughts. The early Greeks, however, believed that the gods were responsible for these natural occurrences and that the gods determined the success or failure of their crops and the health and sickness in their families.

In approximately 700 B.C., 100 years before the first philosophers, the famous Greek poet Homer, author of the *Iliad* and the *Odyssey*, put many myths into writing. He described the scene of Mount Olympus where gods such as Zeus, Apollo, Hero, Athena, and Dionysius lived very similar lives to humans on Earth. These superhuman gods, known as the Homeric gods, ate, drank, and amused themselves. As egoistic and devious as mortals, they were also open to bribery. Because the gods were powerful and even spiteful when angry, the Greeks feared them. The Greeks believed these gods would punish people for their greed, their pride, and their immoral actions. Homer's gods were not always moral themselves, but they were more powerful than humans and demanded obedience from humans. Thus, if a farmer's crops failed, the farmer believed that he had displeased the gods. If there was an illness in the family, the family believed that the gods were getting revenge for their lack of obedience.

Hesiod, a Greek poet who lived about 700 B.C., uses Homer in his writings *Works and Days* to praise the power of Zeus:

> Through him mortal men are famed or unfamed, sung or unsung alike, as great Zeus wills.
>
> For easily he makes strong, and easily he brings the strong man low; easily he humbles the proud and raises the obscure, and easily he straightens the crooked and blasts the proud. . . .
>
> For those who practice violence and cruel deeds far-seeing Zeus . . . ordains a punishment. Often even a whole city suffers for a bad man who sins . . . and lays

great trouble upon the people, famine and plague together, so that the men perish away, and their women
do not bear children, and houses become few. [1]

The pre-Socratics questioned Homer's poetic accounts of
the gods. They also questioned Hesiod's contention that heaven
and Earth consisted of a god and goddess locked in an embrace
until their son forced them apart.

THE FIRST PHILOSOPHERS

The aim of the first philosophers was to find natural, or scientific,
explanations instead of supernatural, or divine, explanations for
the world and its processes. The original Western philosophers
lived in Miletus, a Greek town in Ionia located across the Aegean
Sea from Athens, Greece, in 600 B.C.

The Milesian philosophers were known as natural philosophers because their aim was to find natural instead of supernatural explanations for the world and the way it works. They
were also known as the first materialists. They asked questions
such as, "What is the world made of?" and, "How can we explain
that everything in nature is always changing?" They wanted to
find out if there was a source from which all things came and to
which all things returned. The Milesians wanted to understand
the laws of nature.

These pre-Socratic philosophers discovered that change is
possible only if there is some permanent source or substance
that causes the world to exist. Without this permanent substance, each change would completely replace another, and
nothing could be held together. For example, you are the same
person now as you were when you were born. Yet your body,
your emotions, your mind, your needs, and your interests have
changed. Why is it, then, that you can look at your baby photo-
graph and say, "There I am at six months old?" Everything about

you has changed, yet you are the same person you were at six months. Is there something about you that is permanent? What is this "I" or "you" that does not change?

These natural philosophers wanted to understand change and permanence by studying nature itself, not by reading or listening to stories about the gods. They speculated that all things arise from the same substance, take different forms at different times, and then return again to the same substance. This pre-Socratic reasoning shows a major shift from the mythical explanation for the origins of the cosmos.

Only fragments of what these natural philosophers said and wrote have survived. In fact, most of our information about the pre-Socratics comes from the writings of Aristotle, who lived two centuries later. According to him, the first philosopher in the Western world was Thales.

Miletus was the ancient Greek home of the earliest Western philosophers. The city lies in present-day Turkey. The Miletus theater (above), built by the Greeks in about 300 B.C., was later used by the Romans after their conquest of the Greek empire.

Thales

Thales (c. 624–546 B.C.) is known as the Father of Western Philosophy. He was from Miletus. Thales was the first to ask the questions, "Out of what substance is the world made?" and, "Is there anything permanent that underlies all change?" His answer to both questions was water. Water, he said, is the basic substance of everything in nature. All things have moisture, so water also must be the permanent substance that holds everything together. Thales may have meant that life originated from water and life returned to water again, just as water turns to ice or vapor and then turns back into water again.

Olive Presses

Aristotle relates a story about Thales's scheme for making money. Although known as one of the wisest men in Greece, people mocked Thales for living in poverty, saying, "If you're so smart, why aren't you rich?" and, "What good is philosophy if you can't use it to make money?" Thales explained to these people that money was of little interest to him, but he was sure he could be wealthy if he put his mind to it. They challenged him to become rich, and he accepted their challenge.

From his knowledge of meteorology, Thales observed there would be an excellent crop of olives during the autumn season. In the middle of summer, he rented all the olive presses in Miletus for a small sum of money. When the people saw stacks and stacks of olive presses around his small house during the summer when there were no olives, they made fun at his craziness. However, when autumn came, the olive growers needed presses to make olive oil. Few could be found because Thales had bought them all. Thales then rented the presses to the growers for a huge profit. The farmers grumbled because of his high prices, but he made a lot of money, proving that philosophers could become rich if they chose. Then, he reminded the people that wealth is not the business in which philosophers are interested.

The Sun and the Pyramids

A scientist and mathematician as well as a philosopher, Thales was the first Greek to predict the eclipse of the Sun on May 28, 585 B.C. He was also the first to introduce Egyptian geometry to Greece. Before Thales, the height of the Egyptian pyramids was unknown. Aware of Thales's reputation in mathematics, the Egyptian pharaoh asked Thales if he could conceive a way to measure the height of the pyramids. In those days, mathematicians and scientists did not have the sophisticated tools that we have today. Some had tried to measure the pyramids, but no one had found an accurate way to measure the huge structures. Thales agreed to try, and he thought carefully about a solution. One day, while standing in the Sun looking at a pyramid, he realized that at a certain time of day his own shadow was the exact length of his body. He had his answer. Thales measured a pyramid's shadow at that same time of day to determine the true height of the pyramids.

Anaximander

A student of Thales, Anaximander (c. 612–c. 545 B.C.), also from Miletus, agreed with his teacher that there is some permanent substance that underlies all change, but he disagreed that this substance was water. Water, he said, is within all things, but it is only one among many other elements such as earth, air, and fire. All limited elements—water, earth, air, and fire—must have their origin in something unlimited—something "boundless."

The Boundless

For Anaximander, the unlimited boundless is defined as eternal motion. This motion is not created by anything, not sustained by anything, nor will it ever end. Because of its eternal motion, water and other elements in the boundless separate and come into existence. For example, hot and cold separated and became moisture. From moisture came air and then earth. The boundless, Anaximander argued, produces everything.

Evolution

Anaximander was the first Western philosopher to propose the idea of evolution. Although the word evolution had yet to be invented, he reasoned that humans developed from fish:

> While other animals quickly find food by themselves, man alone requires a lengthy period of suckling. Hence, had he been originally as he is now, he would never have survived. . . .
>
> At first human beings arose in the inside of fishes, and after having been reared like sharks, and become capable of protecting themselves, they were finally cast ashore and took to land.[2]

Anaximenes

Anaximenes (c. 585–c. 525 B.C.) is the third and last well-known philosopher from the Milesian school. Anaximenes thought the substance that holds everything together was not water or the boundless, but air. Air, he said, is everywhere, but unlike Anaximander's boundless, air is a tangible material substance. He believed that Thales's water actually came from condensed air. Air is breath, wind, mind, and soul. As a mathematician, he reasoned that water is condensed air, earth is condensed water, and fire is rarefied air. Thus, air is the origin of earth, water, and fire, and air holds everything together.

Just as our soul, being air, holds us together, so do breath and air encompass the whole world.

When it [air] is dilated so as to be rarer, it becomes fire; while winds, on the other hand, are condensed Air. Cloud is formed from Air by felting [pressing together]; and this, still further condensed, becomes water. Water condensed still more, turns to earth and when condensed as much as it can be to stones. [3]

NEW WAYS OF LOOKING AT THE WORLD

The Milesian philosophers were the first to raise the question about the ultimate nature of things. Considered the first scientists as well as the first philosophers, they believed that a single basic substance is the source of all things. Because they identified this single substance as water, the boundless, and air, we call their philosophy monistic materialism, or theories about the universe based on one material.

As natural philosophers, the Milesians were interested in the physical world. They did not inquire into the nature of human knowledge, nor did they ask about the relation between spirit and body. Now, however, a philosopher named Pythagoras entered the scene. Though he did not follow traditional Greek religious rituals, he did create a spiritual community based on mathematics and spirituality.

Pythagoras

Pythagoras (c. 570–c. 490 B.C.) was the first pre-Socratic to call attention to the mathematical structure of the universe rather than to its substance. Born on the island of Samos in the Aegean Sea just off the coast of Miletus, he felt discontented with the tyrannical rulers and moved to Crotona in southern Italy. There, he founded a society that combined science, religion, music, and mathematics into a philosophy that went beyond the naturalistic outlook of the Milesians. Pythagoras was the first to call himself a *philosopher*, literally meaning a "lover of wisdom."

Number

Pythagoras was the first to distinguish triangular numbers, square numbers, rectangular numbers, and spherical numbers as odd and even. By saying all things have odd or even numbers, Pythagoras could explain opposites such as one and many, straight and curved, rest and motion, and light and dark. As a result of his mathematical figuring, he also discovered a critical geometrical formula that we still use today. Called the Pythagorean theorem, it states that, in a right triangle, the square of the hypotenuse is equal to the squares of the other two sides.

Pythagoras said, "All things are number." To illustrate this argument, he compared the human body to a musical instrument. When the body is "in tune," he said, it is healthy. Disease is the result of tension, the "improper tuning" of the strings. By using numbers, he put together a concept of form. The term *form* meant "limit" or "structure," and numbers represented the use of form to the "unlimited" (Anaximander's boundless). As a result, Pythagoras argued the universe is made up of figures, relationships, and forms.

The Harmonic Mean

Through his studies in mathematics and music, Pythagoras discovered what he called the "harmonic mean." He found that the musical intervals between notes could be expressed in numerical terms of ratios of the numbers one through four. The lengths of the strings of a musical instrument are in direct proportion to the interval of sounds they produce. In other words, a string that makes a sound one octave lower than another string is twice as long as the other string. In this way, he combined mathematics and music. Pythagoras also believed that music is food for the soul. Music is the best medicine to help the diseased person regain harmony, he said.

Three Classes of People

According to Pythagoras, people tend to fall into three classes: (1) lovers of gain; (2) lovers of honor; and (3) lovers of knowledge or wisdom. Pythagoras compared these types of people with those who attended the ancient Olympic Games:

1. The lovers of gain are people who set up booths to sell souvenirs and make money.
2. The lovers of honor are the athletes who compete in the games for honor and fame.
3. The lovers of knowledge are the spectators who show little interest in either money or fame.

The third class of people consists of philosophers who seek knowledge through music and mathematics to help purify and develop harmony of the soul.

This illustration of Pythagoras at work while being observed by a young child was painted by the famous Italian artist Rafaello Sanzio, or Rafael, who was known for the delicacy and grace of his work. The painting was created in about 1510–1512.

Rebirth

Pythagoras viewed the universe with the eye of a mystic, or one who believes that everything in the universe is interrelated and divine. Like the Eastern philosophers, he believed in reincarnation, or the rebirth of a soul in a new human body. The soul, he said, is immortal and passes through many cycles of birth, death, and rebirth. Each human life depends on the kind of life the soul leads in its present life. For example, if one cheats in this life and gets away with it, in the next life, people may cheat on that person. Alternatively, if one is considerate of people in this life, in the next life, people will be considerate of that person. The end goal for all humans is to reach liberation from the birth, death, and rebirth cycle by attaining wisdom.

Rules of Purification

Pythagoras devised rules of purification that people should follow to help purify the mind and body. Among the rules of purification were:

1. Abstain from eating beans.
2. Do not pick up what has fallen.
3. Do not break bread.
4. Do not step over a crossbar.
5. Do not stir the fire with iron.
6. Do not eat from a whole loaf.
7. Do not eat the heart.
8. Do not walk on highways.
9. Do not let swallows share one's roof.
10. When you rise from the bedclothes, roll them together and Smooth[e] out the impress of the body. [4]

Aesara of Lucania

Although Greece was predominately male oriented, a few of Pythagoras's students were female. One outstanding woman philosopher was Aesara of Lucania who thought that, by understanding the soul, we could better understand morality. In her book, *On Human Nature*, she wrote that the orderly soul is just and moral. With this knowledge, we can create a just society.

> Being threefold, [the soul] is organized in accordance with triple functions: that which effects judgment and thoughtfulness is [the mind] ... that which effects strength and ability is [spirited] . . . and that which effects love and kindliness is desire. These are all so disposed relatively to one another that the best part is in command, the most inferior part is governed, and the one in between holds a middle place, it both governs and is governed. [5]

Heraclitus

Heraclitus (c. 540–c. 480 B.C.) was another pre-Socratic philosopher who attempted to answer the questions, "Out of what substance is the world made?" and, "Does something permanent underlie this world of change?" Additionally, Heraclitus wanted to solve the problem of change itself. He came up with the idea that change is constant. Everything is always changing.

Not much is known of Heraclitus's life. Legend has it that he was born into a noble family and gave up his kingship to his younger brother. This legend could be based on the traditional belief of philosophers' disinterest in worldly affairs, or it could be based on Heraclitus's statement, "The kingdom is a child's."

Divine Fire

Unlike Thales, who said the underlying substance of everything in nature is water, and Anaximenes, who believed it was air,

Heraclitus claimed that the substance that holds everything together is fire. He believed that "this world, which is the same for all, no one of gods or men has made; but it was ever, is now, and ever shall be an ever-living Fire, with measures of it kindling, and measures going out." [6]

Heraclitus was not speaking of physical fire such as the fire that causes a log to burn in a campfire. He viewed fire as the substance that keeps the world unified, instead of flying apart in all directions. Fire, for Heraclitus, was divine fire in the sense that it was everywhere, and it affects the world at all times.

State of Flux

Heraclitus believed everything in our world is always changing. In fact, nothing in the world is permanent except for the process of change. Change is the most basic characteristic of nature, and one of Heraclitus's most famous statements is, "All things are in a state of flux." To him, we "cannot step twice into the same river." When we step into the river for the second time, we are not the same and neither is the river, "for new waters ever flow in upon us."

The Play of Opposites

Nature relies on the relationship of opposites. For example, we have day and night, winter and summer, war and peace, pleasure and pain. If we never experienced hunger, we would take no pleasure in being full. If there were no war, we would not appreciate peace. If there were only night, we could not appreciate day. Without winter, we would not experience summer.

Heraclitus looked at the opposites that exist in nature and made a comparison to an archer's bow. The bent bow, said Heraclitus, seems at rest, but only because the string and bow pull equally against each other. Likewise, in nature, rest is the appearance of equal and opposite forces. This relationship of opposites brings balance to the universe. For example, if the strings of a guitar are too tight or too loose, there can be no harmony. The strings must have the correct tension for a harmonious sound to come from the guitar.

God Is Reason

For Heraclitus, fire is God's universal Logos. Logos can be defined as reason, or the structure and the order of the universe. God, as the source of Logos, guides everything that happens in nature and holds everything together. "God [universal reason] is day and night, winter and summer, war and peace, hunger and satiety," Heraclitus said. God is in everything. Because God is Logos, and Logos is reason, or the ability to think clearly and logically, and the human soul is part of God, we humans have the capacity to think. Although we do not always think alike or have the same abilities to reason, Heraclitus believed that God's "universal reason" guides everything that happens in nature. Just as nature obeys natural laws, human beings should live according to rational rules, such as moral principles—by telling the truth, keeping promises, showing loyalty to friends, and, of course, striving for philosophical wisdom. Only through such morality can we find happiness. Heraclitus showed his contempt for people who would rather follow pleasures of the physical senses than follow reason, when he said, "Asses would rather have straw than gold," and, "Fools when they do hear are like the deaf: Of them does the saying bear witness that they are absent when present."

THE ELEATICS

One of the most interesting aspects of philosophy is the different ways philosophers have of approaching the same problem. Following Pythagoras and Heraclitus were two philosophers from the Greek colony of Elea in southern Italy. These "Eleatics," as they were called, were interested in the question of change, just as the previous pre-Socratic philosophers were. Yet, the Eleatics came to far different conclusions than the pre-Socratics. Two of the most important Eleatics were Parmenides, who founded the Eleatic School of philosophy, and his student, Zeno.

Parmenides

In contrast to Pythagoras, Heraclitus, and the Milesian philosophers, Parmenides (c. 540–c. 480 B.C.) said there is no such thing as change. Parmenides set forth his philosophy in his poem "On Nature." He considered the physical senses as deceptive and argued that sensible things were mere illusion, giving us false information. The question he asked was, "How does the One, or substance, change into the many (sensible things) that we experience in everyday experience?"

For Parmenides, the only true being is the One, which is infinite and indivisible. The One is not, as Heraclitus believed, a union of opposites, because there are no opposites, according to Parmenides. What now exists, Parmenides said, always existed. Nothing can come from nothing, and nothing that exists can become nothing. "What is, *is*. What is not, is not," he posited. What is, is everlasting 'Being', the true reality. Therefore, Being cannot change into what is not (non-Being), and what is not cannot change into what is. Therefore, Parmenides reasoned, there can be no such thing as change.

Parmenides argued that whatever is, is 1) uncreated; 2) indestructible; 3) eternal; and 4) unchangeable. His arguments to support that nothing changes are reconstructed as follows:

(1) What is, is uncreated. In order to prove this let us assume its opposite, namely, that what is[,] was created. If what is, was created it must have been created either (a) out of nothing[,] or (b) out of something. But (a) it could

not be created out of nothing, for there is no nothing; and (b) we cannot say that it was created out of something, for, on the assumption of monism, there is no "something else"—there is only what is. This exhausts the possibilities; Since something is neither created (a) out of nothing[,] nor (b) out of something, it is uncreated.

Again (2) what is, is indestructible. Destruction of anything would involve its disappearance (change into nothing), and there is no nothing.

It follows that (3) what is, is eternal, for what is uncreated and indestructible is obviously eternal.

(4) What is, is unchangeable. This follows in the first place, from the argument about indestructibility. What we mean by change is a transformation into something else. When a thing is transformed into something else, it becomes what it was not (the old thing disappears; the new thing appears). But there is no nothing for the old thing to disappear into. [7]

Briefly, then, Parmenides holds:
(1) There is no change because change is the coming into being of what was not.
(2) Therefore, the senses are an illusion.

You may object to Parmenides's theory by saying, "I can see with my naked eye that things around me are always changing." Yet, Parmenides would answer, "You think reality is based on sense experience. Our senses do not give us an accurate picture of the world. Even though our senses tell us that things change, our reason tells us that reality must be permanent; thus, there is no change."

Many Eastern and Western philosophers agree with Parmenides that true reality is permanent, and the world of our senses is only partially accurate. For instance, would the principle of Truth or the principle of Goodness ever change? Our understanding of Truth and Goodness may change, but does Truth change? Does Goodness change? If we hold a stick in the water, the stick appears bent to our eyes, but our reason tells us it is not really bent. Which is correct, our reason or our senses? Are both correct?

At age 65, Parmenides traveled to Athens, Greece, accompanied by his student Zeno. On this visit, Parmenides discussed philosophy with the young Socrates. Years later, Plato, an admirer of Parmenides's thinking, wrote a dialogue called *Parmenides*, which provides us with an account of the conversation between Parmenides and Socrates. Some Greek philosophers, however, criticized Parmenides's argument that nothing changes, so Zeno took it upon himself to defend his teacher's position.

Zeno

As a member of the Eleatic school, Zeno (c. 490–c. 430 B.C.) tried to prove Parmenides's concept that there is no change with mathematics. He pointed out that contradiction results if we think that change is possible. His famous argument is that of Achilles and the tortoise. The argument intends to prove that contrary to what the senses see—and no matter how fast Achilles runs—he never overtakes the slow, crawling tortoise.

The Racecourse

Achilles, the fastest of all runners in Greek mythology, is about to race with a tortoise. A good sport, Achilles gives the tortoise a head start. Once that is done, said Zeno, Achilles can never overtake the tortoise because he must always reach the point the tortoise has passed. Because the distance between Achilles and the tortoise will always be divisible, no point on the racecourse can be reached before the previous point has been reached.

> You cannot cross a race-course. You cannot traverse an infinite number of points in a finite time. You must traverse the half of any given distance before you traverse the whole, and the half of that again before you can traverse the whole, and the half of that again before you can traverse it. This goes on ad infinitum [forever], so that there are an infinite number of points in any given space, and you cannot touch an infinite number one by one in a finite time. [8]

Zeno's conclusion was that there could be no motion at all. Because there is no motion, Achilles could never overtake the tortoise. Therefore, Being is the one true reality, and change and motion are only illusions. As Zeno writes, "Achilles will never overtake the tortoise. He must first reach the place from which the tortoise started. By that time the tortoise will have got some way ahead. Achilles must then make up that, and again the tortoise will be ahead. He is always coming nearer, but he never makes up to it." [9]

Zeno wanted us to give up the belief that any kind of division or change is possible, which also forces us to give up the belief that our senses provide us with knowledge. Zeno's argument remains one of the most famous but also remains one of the most difficult paradoxes in philosophy.

THE PLURALISTS

Heraclitus and Parmenides had perceived the world in opposite ways. Heraclitus argued that nature is in a constant state of change; everything flows, and our sensory perceptions are reliable. Parmenides, taking the opposite view, believed that there is no change; our sensory perceptions are unreliable. The pluralists agreed with Heraclitus that change is a fact. Yet, they also agreed with Parmenides that Being is, and Being does not change.

The pluralists believed that Heraclitus, Parmenides, and the Milesians were wrong for assuming the presence of only one element or substance—fire for Heraclitus, Being for Parmenides, water for Thales, the boundless for Anaximander, and air for Anaximenes.

The pluralists contended that, if we accepted these conclusions, we would have no bridge between what we see with our senses and what our reason tells us. The source of nature, the pluralists concluded, cannot possibly be one single element. Instead, the source should consist of many elements, hence the name, *pluralists*. These thinkers set out to find the bridge between the mind and the senses by finding the many elements that are the source of nature.

Empedocles

Empedocles (c. 490–c. 430 B.C.), a poet and doctor as well as a philosopher, was from Agrigentum, Sicily. His interests ranged from medicine and philosophy to religion and politics. A colorful figure and a believer in rebirth, Empedocles believed all souls could not die.

In fact, he introduced himself to his fellow citizens as "an immortal god, no longer subject to death." His desire to be remembered as godlike gave rise to the belief that he ended his life by leaping into the crater of the volcano on Mount Etna, hoping to leave no trace of his body so that people would think he had gone up to heaven. In the humorous words of a poet:

> *Great Empedocles that ardent soul leapt*
> *Into Etna, and was roasted whole.*

The Four Elements

Reality is not just one substance or element, said Empedocles. Reality is a plurality of elements: earth, air, fire, and water. When these four elements combine, they form everything in the world, including human beings, animals, flowers, rocks, mountains, and the ocean. The four elements are "the roots of all" that exists, claimed Empedocles. When a tree or an animal dies, the four elements separate. We can see these changes with the naked eye, but the four true elements are eternal and unchanging. They continually combine and separate in different proportions, yet they always remain earth, air, fire, and water. Thus, something about these elements changes, yet something remains the same.

Love and Strife

Empedocles struggled with the question, "What causes the four elements to combine and to separate?" He concluded that two processes caused the combination and separation of the elements—love and strife. Love brings the elements together, and strife separates them. Without love, everything falls apart.

> I shall tell thee a twofold tale. At one time it grew to be one only out of many; at another, it divided up to be many instead of one. There is a double becoming of perishable things and a double passing away. The coming together of all things brings one generation into being and destroys it; the other grows up and is scattered as things become divided. And these things never cease continually changing places, at one time all uniting in one through Love, at another each borne in different directions by the repulsion of strife. Thus, as far as it is their nature to grow into one out of many, and to become many once more when the one is parted asunder, so far they come into being and their life abides not.

But, inasmuch as they never cease changing their places continually, so far they are ever immovable as they go round the circle of existence. [10]

Anaxagoras

Anaxagoras (c. 500–c. 428 B.C.) was born in Clazomenae, Ionia, on the coast of Asia Minor. In about 480 B.C., he moved to Athens, where he was later tried and condemned on a charge of atheism. Saved by his friend, the great Athenian statesman Pericles, Anaxagoras went into exile at Lampsacus, a Milesian colony. He was the first philosopher to make a distinction between Mind, or *nous*, and matter.

Anaxagoras agreed with Empedocles that everything is a mixture of earth, air, fire, and water, but he rejected love and strife as the forces that combine and separate things. Furthermore, he did not agree with the Milesians that one single substance could be the basic substance made into everything we see in nature.

Seeds

Anaxagoras believed there are an infinite number of tiny, invisible particles that are the building blocks of nature. He called these minuscule particles that carry the blueprint of everything else "seeds."

Mind, or Nous

For Anaxagoras, the mind, or intelligence, produces the orderly structure of the world. Love and strife do not combine or separate things in an orderly pattern; it is the nous that allows for the structure of the world.

And Nous had power over the whole revolution, so that it began to revolve in the beginning. . . . And all the things that are mingled together and separated off and distinguished are all known by Nous. And Nous set in order all things that were to be, and all things that were and are not now and that are, and this revolution in which now revolve not now and that are, and this revolution in which now revolve the stars and the sun and the moon, and the air and the aether that are separated off. And this revolution caused the separating off, and the rare is separated off from the dense, the warm from the cold, the light from the dark, and the dry from the moist. And there are many portions in many things. [11]

Anaxagoras, shown in this eighteenth-century engraving, used his observations about celestial bodies to develop new theories about the order of the universe.

Mind animates everything in nature and is present in all living things—the Sun, stars, Earth, plants, and humans. Mind does not create matter because matter is eternal. Yet, Mind does bring order to matter, because Mind has all knowledge about everything. Mind is the "finest of all things and the purest," Anaxagoras claimed. By distinguishing Mind from matter, but not necessarily separating Mind from matter, Anaxagoras was to influence philosophers for generations to come.

The Sun

The Sun, said Anaxagoras, is not a god, but a red-hot stone, bigger than Greece's Peloponnesian peninsula. From his studies in astronomy, he found that all heavenly bodies are made of the same materials as Earth and that the Moon produces no light of its own; its light comes from Earth. These statements so upset the Athenians that they accused him of being an atheist and forced him to leave the city. He sailed across the Aegean Sea to the city of Lampsacus where he became a schoolteacher. For centuries after his death, Lampsacus celebrated his birthday as a school holiday.

THE ATOMISTS

The last of the pre-Socratics who gave their answers to Thales's question, "Out of what substance is everything made?" are the atomists Leucippus and Democritus. These philosophers formulated a theory about the nature of things that bears a surprising similarity to some of today's scientific views. The atomists agreed with their predecessors that there must be something permanent in nature, something that underlies all change and holds everything together. Yet, the atomists held different ideas about what this permanent something is. They reasoned that everything in nature was made of tiny, invisible particles, or units, called "atoms."

Leucippus

Scholars consider Leucippus the founder of the atomistic school and a speculative thinker of the highest degree. Yet, scholars give Democritus the credit for working out the detailed application of the theory. We have very little biographical data for Leucippus. Some scholars doubt that he ever existed, but Aristotle and others refute this notion. In fact, in his work entitled *Of Generation and Corruption*, Aristotle discussed many of Leucippus's atomistic ideas. Leucippus was probably born in Miletus, a younger contemporary of Anaxagoras, and his main philosophical teaching probably occurred between 450–420 B.C.

Democritus

One of the most important atomists, Democritus (c. 460–c. 370 B.C.) lived in Abdera, a city in Thrace in northern Greece. He wrote as many as 52 books, of which over 200 fragments have been preserved.

Atoms

The word *atom* means "uncuttable." The atomists thought atoms could not be divided into smaller parts because if they were, nature would eventually dissolve and disappear. Leucippus and Democritus described atoms as hard and indivisible, with different shapes and sizes, yet invisible to the naked eye. The different shapes of the atoms allow them to join together into all kinds of different bodies. When a human body, a flower, or an animal dies, the atoms scatter and later come together again to form new bodies.

While Pythagoras posited that all things are numbers, the atomists believed everything is a combination of atoms. Parmenides, by saying there is only Being and no nonbeing, concluded that there could be no empty space because space would be nothing, and there is no nothing. Democritus opposed Parmenides's idea that there is no empty space. For Democritus, there is infinite empty space. He said the universe is made up of:

> atoms and empty space; everything else is merely thought to exist. The worlds are unlimited; they come into being and perish. Nothing can come into being from that which is not nor pass away into that which is not. Further the atoms are unlimited in size and number, and they are borne along in the whole universe in a vortex, and thereby generate all composite things—it is because of their solidity that these atoms are impassive and unalterable. The sun and the moon have been composed of such smooth and spherical masses, and so also the soul, which is identical with reason. We see by virtue of the impact of images upon our eyes. All things happen by virtue of necessity, the vortex being the cause of the creation of all things. [12]

The atomists reasoned that everything in nature results from the collision of atoms moving in space. They did not believe that a god designed or moved these atoms from place to place. Instead, they thought atoms inherently obeyed the mechanical laws of nature. Because the only things that exist are atoms and empty space, which are material things, we call the atomists "materialists."

Soul Atoms

Democritus believed that our thoughts also result from atoms. In other words, when you see a monkey, it is because "monkey atoms" enter your eyes. Monkey atoms make an impact upon your "soul atoms," and a thought is born. For Democritus, the soul is made up of round, smooth soul atoms. At death, the soul atoms will scatter and could, like body atoms, become part of a new soul formation. This idea suggests there is no personal, immortal soul. For Democritus, the soul, including thought, connects to the brain. Once the brain dies, we cannot have any form of consciousness.

Morality

Although Democritus believed that everything has natural causes and follows the mechanical laws of nature, he believed that we have some control over our thoughts. He developed a set of moral rules that we should use to achieve happiness.

> Not from fear but from a sense of duty refrain from your sins.
>
> He who does wrong is more unhappy than he who suffers wrong.
>
> Strength of body is nobility in beasts of burden, strength of character is nobility in men.
>
> Those who have a well-ordered character lead also a well-ordered life. [13]

LINKS TO THE CLASSICAL PERIOD

In the years after the pre-Socratics, philosophers turned their concentration from the physical world to questions about how we should behave morally. The next great development in philosophy is the classical period. With the exception of Pythagoras and Heraclitus, a group of paid teachers called "Sophists" and the unpaid philosopher Socrates were the first Western philosophers to ask questions about the nature of human beings, their moral problems, and the meaning of life. They struggled with the problems that confront every human being and asked the questions, "Who am I?" "What do I want out of life?" and, "How should I live?" Their findings gave them an important place in the history of science as well as philosophy.

2

THE CLASSICAL PERIOD:
THE SOPHISTS
AND SOCRATES

The unexamined life is not worth living.
—Socrates

The Sophists were skeptical of the pre-Socratics' efforts to find a universal substance. They questioned any human's ability to know the truth about things such as substance, permanence, and change. To prove their point, the Sophists showed how each of the pre-Socratic philosophers disagreed about the universe: Thales said the basic substance was water, Anaximander said it was the boundless, Anaximenes said air, Pythagoras said number, Heraclitus said fire, Parmenides and Zeno said Being, Empedocles said the four root elements, Anaxagoras said Mind, and the atomists said atoms. Consequently, the Sophists turned their attention away from physical elements of nature to the human side of life. They focused on practical, day-to-day problems of people and their societies.

For a while, Socrates was a student of the Sophists, but he disagreed with their skepticism. Socrates believed the human soul has the capacity to know eternal, unchanging elements such as Truth, Beauty, and Goodness. Socrates believed that to gain knowledge of these things is the most important goal of our lives. For Socrates, "The unexamined life is not worth living."

THE SOPHISTS

In approximately 450 B.C., Athens was the cultural center of Greece, in the early stages of Greece's young democracy. For democracy to work, people needed to be educated about the democratic process of government. Before democracy developed in Athens, only males from powerful aristocratic families had the advantage of an education. But after the Persian Wars (449–448 B.C.), Greek businessmen and politicians challenged the privileges of the aristocracy. As the government changed in Athens, any young man who was smart enough and could afford tuition could receive an education. Athenian democracy was perhaps the only real democracy that has ever existed. It had no political parties, nor were there any professional politicians. Any male citizen could address the assembly of the people, and all decisions were made by popular vote. Women and slaves were not considered citizens and therefore could not vote. Slavery was accepted by all ancient societies, but to its credit, Athens was well known for its liberal attitude toward slaves. Women were not educated but expected to live sheltered lives as wives and mothers instead.

With democracy on the rise, a need for lawyers also grew. For the Athenians to speak convincingly in a court of law, it was necessary to master the art of public speaking. Recognizing the need for educators to train lawyers and politicians, a group of teachers and philosophers from neighboring colonies gathered in Athens. They called themselves "Sophists," from a Greek word that means "wise" or "learned," and they made their living charging fees for teaching. The most outstanding Sophists in Athens were Protagoras, Gorgias, and Thrasymachus. These men believed that absolutes such as Truth, Beauty, and Goodness do not exist in this world. Because right and wrong are relative to a culture, the "good life" depends on the particular situation. In philosophy, this viewpoint is known as relativism. Relativists believe each society should make its own rules.

The Sophists taught young lawyers how to argue court cases regardless of their clients' guilt or innocence. Young politicians learned the art of using fallacies, or misleading arguments, and emotional language to benefit their cause. The Sophists taught their students to present clear, forceful arguments and to attack the logical fallacies in their opponents' arguments. This same type of training has lasted in legal and political circles for more than 2,000 years.

The following story about the Sophist Protagoras and one of his students demonstrates the Sophistic art of persuasion:

A young man who did not have enough money to pay for lessons asked Protagoras to accept him as a law student anyway. Protagoras agreed on the condition that the student would pay when he won his first case. The student agreed, but after he completed the course, the student took no cases. Annoyed, Protagoras took the student to court for payment. The student argued, "If I win this case, I won't have to pay Protagoras according to the judgment of the court. If I lose this case, then I have yet to win my first case, so according to our agreement, win or lose I don't have to pay him." At that point, Protagoras stepped forward to argue his case, claiming, "If he loses this case, then by the judgment of the court, he will have to pay. If he wins this case, he will have won his first case and will have to pay me. In either case he must pay."

Unfortunately, we do not know the outcome of this case, or even if this story is true. Yet, true or false, the story illustrates the art of rhetoric, or the art of speaking persuasively. Because of circumstances such as these, and because the Sophists charged extravagant fees, Socrates called the Sophists "prostitutes of wisdom."

Protagoras

Protagoras (c. 481–c. 411 B.C.), the most famous Sophist in Athens, stated, "Man is the measure of all things." In this statement, he rejected everything the pre-Socratic philosophers thought was true. He denied any ultimate principle or truth that we can know. For Protagoras, truth is relative. For example, if you and I

The wars between Greece and Persia were a series of conflicts referring to the two Persian invasions of Greece in 490 and 480 B.C. Each invasion was successfully turned back by the Greeks. This Greek wine jug from the mid-fifth century is decorated with a Greek and a Persian warrior locked in combat.

disagree, we may both be right depending upon what we believe or what we learned from our culture. "Man is the measure of all things" suggests that our knowledge is dependent upon our sensations, feelings, and perceptions, as well as our reason. In Plato's dialogue *Theaetetus*, Socrates and Theaetetus have the following conversation about Protagoras's statement that "man is the measure of all things."

> *Socrates:* [Protagoras] says . . . that "man is the measure of all things" . . . . He puts it in this sort of way . . . that any given thing "is to me such as it appears to me, and is to you such as it appears to you . . . ?"
>
> *Theaetetus:* Yes, that is how he puts it.
>
> *Socrates:* Let us follow up his meaning. Sometimes, when the same wind is blowing, one of us feels chilly, the other does not, or one may feel slightly chilly, the other quite cold.
>
> *Theaetetus:* Certainly.
>
> *Socrates:* Well, in that case are we to say that the wind in itself is cold or not cold? Or shall we agree with Protagoras that it is cold to the one who feels chilly, and not to the other? [14]

For the Sophists, there is no ultimate knowledge of absolute truth but only knowledge of how things affect us. The wind may feel cold to me and warm to you, but we cannot say the wind is cold or warm itself. Therefore, each of us is correct in our judgment of how the wind seems.

Relativism

Relativism encompasses all walks of life, including religion and morality. Relativism is the belief that what is true and good depends upon the situation. Morality is good when it produces useful results in our life. Each society creates its own moral rules. Thus, there is no ultimate standard of morality for everyone in the world. These relative moral rules also exist in religion. For example, some religions consider drinking alcohol immoral, and other religions say it is permissible to drink alcohol in moderation. Some religions ban certain books and music, and other religions suggest we use discrimination in what we read and listen to. Protagoras believed that the society we live in should make the laws that everyone accepts because those laws are best suited to that particular society.

Gorgias

Gorgias (c. 483–c. 375 B.C.) arrived in Athens as the ambassador of his native city of Leontini, Sicily. Protagoras had said, "Man is the measure of all things." Therefore, because we see things differently, almost anything could be true. Gorgias took the opposite view, arguing that *nothing* is true. Gorgias held that, even if truth exists, we could never prove it, nor could we communicate it to others.

Gorgias also disagreed with Protagoras's argument that we should follow conventional moral rules. Gorgias asked, "if moral rules are merely convention, why should we follow them if they are not to our advantage?"

Because Gorgias was such a firm skeptic, or someone who questions our ability to have knowledge of reality, he gave up the philosophical search for truth and turned to rhetoric, a field in which he was considered a master. In Plato's dialogue *Gorgias*, Gorgias boasts of his skills:

[Rhetoric gives you the power] to convince by your words the judges in court, the senators in Council, the people in the Assembly, or in any other gathering of a citizen body. And yet possessed of such power you will make the doctor, you will make the trainer your slave, and your businessman will prove to be making money, not for himself, but for another, for you who can speak and persuade multitudes.

I have often, along with my brother and with other physicians, visited one of their patients who refused to drink his medicine or submit to the surgeon's knife or cautery [to deaden pain by burning the skin], and when the doctor was unable to persuade them, I did so, by no other art but rhetoric. [15]

Thrasymachus

As we have seen, Protagoras thought citizens should follow the moral rules of their society. Gorgias asked why we would want to follow society's moral rules if they are not going to benefit us. In about 450 B.C., Thrasymachus (c. 459–c. 400 B.C.) advocated the idea of might makes right. Thrasymachus believed that to speak of moral right and wrong makes no sense at all. "Right," said Thrasymachus, "means serving the interest of the stronger who rules, at the cost of the subject who obeys." So, if the unjust person is intelligent, he will be more successful than the just person. Thus, might becomes right when it is to the benefit of the party or person in power.

Take a private business: When a partnership is wound up, you will never find that the more honest of two partners comes off with the larger share; and in their relations to the state, when there are taxes to be paid, the honest man will pay more than the other on the same amount of property; or if there is money to be distributed, the dishonest will get it all. [16]

One influential contemporary of Thrasymachus objected to the idea that the unjust person can be superior. For this thinker, the reason we are here on Earth is to make our souls as good as possible. Everyone wants to be happy, and happiness comes from attaining knowledge of the good and leading a good life. Happiness does not come from power or worldly success, he argued. This is the philosophy of Socrates.

Socrates

Socrates grew up when Athens was at its peak, when the city was the cultural center in the ancient world. Athens had won victories over the Persians and had become a naval power, controlling much of the Mediterranean Sea. The Athenian Navy soon freed the Mediterranean of pirates, thus opening the waterways for commerce to flourish. The Athenian government also had vast wealth, erecting the Parthenon, a monumental temple dedicated to Athena, the goddess of intelligence and patroness of Athens. Never before in history was there a period of such high quality works in architecture, sculpture, and drama, nor had so many great playwrights, poets, artists, and historians lived in the same city. Socrates loved his city and fought bravely in many of Athens's wars with Sparta, another Greek city-state. Socrates spent his days walking the city streets discussing many subjects with anyone willing to converse with him. He was regarded as the wisest man in Athens. However, his challenging questions got him into trouble.

Just as Thales is known as the Father of Western Philosophy, Socrates is considered the Father of Moral Philosophy. The reason for this title has to do with the courage he showed in living an examined life as well as in facing death. Like the Buddha and Jesus, Socrates wrote nothing, yet he is one of the most influential philosophers in history. Socrates said, "The unexamined life is not worth living," and true to his word, he lived a fully examined life.

Because Socrates wrote nothing, most of what we know about him and his philosophy comes from the writings of Xenophon and Plato. Xenophon, a soldier and Greek historian, characterized Socrates as a loyal warrior who could go without food longer than any other soldier. During winter campaigns, while others wore coats and fleece-lined boots, Socrates wore only a light tunic and sandals. Each morning before sunrise, he would meditate. After the Sun rose, he would give thanks to God and go about his daily duties. One time, Socrates stood for 24 hours in a meditative trance. He did not eat or drink, nor did he move from the spot of his meditation. During this 24-hour period, he discovered his mission in life:

The Parthenon was built in the fifth century B.C. on the hill of the Acropolis, or "high city" of Athens. Adorned with dozens of sculptures, many now gone, the Parthenon is a lasting symbol of ancient Greece, and is often regarded as the highest achievement in Greek art.

Like the Prophets, he was certain of his calling; unlike them, he had nothing to proclaim. No God had chosen him to tell men what He commanded. His mission was only to search in the company of men, himself a man among men. To question unrelentingly, to expose every hiding place. To demand no faith in anything or in himself, but to demand thought, questioning, testing, and so refer man to his own self. But since man's self resides solely in the knowledge of the true and the good, only the man who takes such thinking seriously, who is determined to be guided by the truth, is truly himself. [17]

Most of what we know about Socrates's teachings comes to us through the dialogues of Plato. In these dialogues, Plato used Socrates as his main character and mouthpiece. Plato portrayed Socrates as a man with great courage and moral purity.

Socrates's Life

Socrates (469–399 B.C.) was born in Athens, Greece, and lived there all of his life. His mother was a midwife, and his father was a sculptor or a stonemason. Little is known of Socrates's life before his service in the military. Physically, Socrates was quite ugly. He had a potbelly, bulging eyes, a snub nose, and a squat build. Yet, he was a delightful man. Socrates used to laugh at his own appearance, and more than once, he announced plans to "dance off" his belly. His interests, however, had nothing to do with his physical characteristics. Virtue, he said, is inner goodness, and real beauty is that of the soul, not the body.

Socrates's Inner Voice

Even as a youngster, Socrates had listened to an "inner voice" that he called his "daimon." "I have had this from my childhood; it is a sort of voice that comes to me, and when it comes it always holds me back from what I am thinking of doing, but never urges me forward." When he thought of going into politics, the voice said no. His daimon gave Socrates no instructions about what he should do, but always forbade him to do anything that would have evil consequences. Socrates always obeyed the voice, even if he did not understand why it said no.

The Oracle at Delphi

The ancient Greeks consulted the Oracle at Delphi, a town in Greece, about important problems. Pythia, the priestess presiding over the Oracle, would go into a trance to allow Apollo, the god of the Oracle, to channel messages though her.

One day, Chaerophon, a friend of Socrates, asked the Oracle at Delphi, "Who is the wisest of men?" The Oracle answered, "Socrates." When Chaerophon told Socrates what the Oracle had said, Socrates was astonished. He knew the Oracle never lied, but he also felt that he was not wise. So he decided to question people in Athens who were considered knowledgeable. He questioned priests, poets, politicians, businessmen, and craftsmen, hoping to discover why the Oracle had called him the wisest of men.

Finally, the true meaning of the Oracle dawned on him. The people he had questioned were ignorant of what is most important to know: how to make their souls as good as possible. Only Socrates realized the importance of this knowledge, but he was also aware of his ignorance of it. The people he questioned thought they knew when they really did not know. Socrates concluded that he was at least the "one-eyed" in a "kingdom of the blind." He was the wisest because he was the only one who knew he did *not* know.

The Socratic Method

Socrates always insisted that he was not a teacher but instead acted as a "kind of midwife." Just as a midwife aids a pregnant mother in giving birth, Socrates helped "pregnant souls" give birth to the knowledge hidden within them. Instead of lecturing, he asked questions and questioned answers. He allowed no one to sidestep an answer. Socrates did not believe we are born with blank minds that our teachers, parents, and peers fill with information. He believed souls have the hidden knowledge of Truth, Beauty, and Goodness. Yet, when we get caught up in worldly affairs, as most people do, this wisdom is forgotten. So Socrates asked questions to help individuals realize what they already knew. With this procedure, Socrates invented the dialectic method of finding truth through conversation, also known as the Socratic method.

Plato's dialogue *Euthyphro* is a good example of the dialectic method. Socrates meets the young man Euthyphro on the courthouse steps. Euthyphro asks why Socrates is there. Socrates tells Euthyphro he has been charged with impiety, or lacking respect or reverence, or being impious. Euthyphro then explains that he is suing his own father for impiety. "Really," says Socrates, "then perhaps you can tell me what impiety is." Euthyphro tries to explain, but through Socrates's questioning, Euthyphro realizes that he does not have a clear idea of the meaning of piety or impiety.

> *Socrates:* Well then Euthyphro, what do we say about piety? Is it not loved by all the gods, according to your definition?
>
> *Euthyphro:* Yes.
>
> *Socrates:* Because it is pious, or for some other reason?
>
> *Euthyphro:* No, because it is pious.
>
> *Socrates:* Then it is loved by the gods because it is pious; it is not pious because it is loved by them?
>
> *Euthyphro:* It seems so.

Socrates: But, then, what is pleasing to the gods is pleasing to them, and is in a state of being loved by them, because they love it?

Euthyphro: Of course.

Socrates: Then piety is not what is pleasing to the gods, and what is pleasing to the gods is not pious, as you say, Euthyphro. They are different things.

Euthyphro: And why, Socrates?

Socrates: Because we are agreed that the gods love piety because it is pious, and that it is not pious because they love it. Is not this so?

Euthyphro: Yes.

Socrates: And that what is pleasing to the gods because they love it is pleasing to them by reason of this same love, and that they do not love it because it is pleasing to them.

Euthyphro: True.

Socrates: Then, my dear Euthyphro, piety and what is pleasing to the gods are different things. If the gods had loved piety because it is pious, they would also have loved what is pleasing to them because it is pleasing to them; but if what is pleasing to them had been pleasing to them because they loved it, then piety, too, would have been piety because they loved it. But now you see that they are opposite things, and wholly different from each other. For the one is of a sort to be loved because it is loved, while the other is loved because it is of a sort to be loved. My question, Euthyphro, was, What is piety? But it turns out that you have not explained to me the essential character of piety; you have been content to mention an effect which belongs to it—namely, that all the gods love it. You have not yet told me what its essential character is. Do not, if you please, keep me from what piety is; begin again and tell me that. Never mind whether the gods love it, or whether it has other effects; we shall not differ on that point. Do your best to make clear to me what is piety and what is impiety.

Euthyphro: But, Socrates, I really don't know how to explain to you what is in my mind. Whatever statement we put forward always somehow moves round in a circle, and will not stay where we put it. [18]

Before Socrates had finished the questioning, Euthyphro said, "Another time, then, Socrates. I am in a hurry now, and it is time for me to be off." Euthyphro's response tells us that Socrates's dialectical method was not always welcome. In some cases, pregnant souls were not ready to give birth.

Socrates continually urged people to discover the difficulties in concepts that seemed to be self-evident. For instance, in the Declaration of Independence, America's Founding Fathers wrote that "all men are created equal" was a truth that was self-evident. Socrates would want to know how we were created and what exactly the Founding Fathers meant by "equal."

Moral Philosophy

Socrates said that our most important goal in life is "to make the soul as good as possible." Only knowledge of the soul will lead us to living the good life. Unlike the Sophists, he did not believe that any of us would consciously choose evil over good because we always seek our own well-being. For example, have you ever lied to protect yourself? Have you ever cheated on a test? Socrates would say we do these things because we think the results of these actions will benefit us. Yet, could lying and cheating ever benefit us? No, said Socrates. We do bad things because we are ignorant of what is truly good. He warns us that the guilt of our soul is harder on us than any supposed gains. Thus, moral virtue is identical with knowledge, and moral evil is identical with our ignorance of moral knowledge.

The Trial of Socrates

Because Socrates examined his own life and urged others to examine theirs, many Athenians considered him dangerous. Young men from influential Athenian families were using Socrates's dialectic method to question traditional customs in politics and religion. So it was not surprising when the politicians Anytus and Meletus, who feared Socrates's questions, brought him to trial. They charged Socrates with failing to worship the gods of the state and corrupting the youth. Socrates's prosecutor, Meletus, demanded the death penalty. Usually, anyone charged with such crimes would voluntarily accept exile as punishment, but Socrates refused to leave his beloved Athens. Instead, he defended himself in front of a court with a jury of 501 male citizens.

Socrates refused to play on the jury's emotions by pleading for mercy or insisting that his wife and children needed him. Instead, he lectured the jury members on their own ignorance. He told the Athenians how lucky they were that the gods made him serve "as a sort of gadfly" to the people, arousing them to examine their lives, just as a pesky fly bothers the livestock it annoys.

The following is an excerpt of Socrates's tongue-in-cheek defense from Plato's dialogue *Apology*.

> And now, Athenians[,] I am not arguing in my own defense at all, as you might expect me to do, but rather in yours in order you may not make a mistake about the gift of the god to you by condemning me. For if you put me to death, you will not easily find another who, if I may use a ludicrous comparison, clings to the state as a

sort of gadfly to a horse that is large and well-bred but rather sluggish because of its size, so that it needs to be aroused. It seems to me that the god has attached me like that to the state, for I am constantly alighting upon you at every point to arouse, persuade, and reproach each of you all day long. You will not easily find anyone else, my friends, to fill my place; and if you are persuaded by me, you will spare my life. You are indignant, as drowsy persons are when they are awakened, and, of course, if you are persuaded by Anytus, you could easily kill me with a single blow, and then sleep on undisturbed for the rest of your lives, unless the god in his care for you sends another to arouse you. [19]

Annoyed by Socrates's defense, the jury found him guilty. Meletus and Anytus once again asked for the death penalty. Yet, first, as was the custom, the jury asked Socrates to suggest an alternative punishment. Perhaps they hoped he would choose to leave Athens or promise never to philosophize again. Socrates, however, disappointed the jurists. In response to his question, "What do I deserve?" Socrates replied:

Something good, Athenians. . . . There is no reward, Athenians, so suitable . . . as receiving free meals in the prytaneum [a public hall in which the community's hospitality was extended to distinguished guests]. It is a much more suitable reward . . . than for any of you who has won a victory at the Olympic games, with his horse or his chariots. Such a man only makes you seem happy, but I make you really happy; he is not in want, and I am. So if I am to propose the penalty which I really deserve, I propose this—free meals in the prytaneum. [20]

Furious, the jury sentenced Socrates to death. Undaunted, Socrates said that his death would do those who accused him unjustly more harm than it would him, for "no harm can come to a good man."

The Death of Socrates

While Socrates was in prison, his friends offered to help him escape, but he refused. He loved Athens and her laws. If he escaped, he would be defying his beloved city. The laws, insisted Socrates, were not responsible for his death—his accusers were.

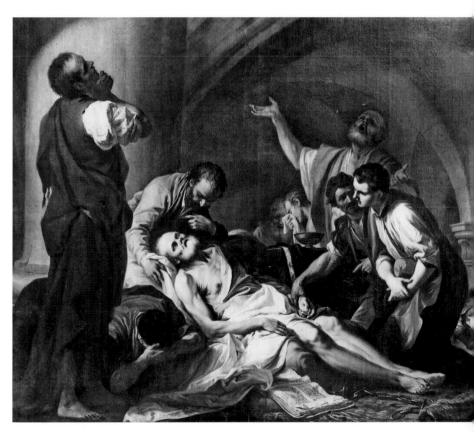

The death of Socrates, shown in this painting by Giambettino Cignaroli from about 1760, has for centuries inspired writers, artists, and philosophers to tell the story of the progressive Athenian thinker who was considered by many to be a danger to their society.

On the day of his execution, Socrates conversed with his family and friends. At sunset, the jailer gave Socrates hemlock, a poisonous herb. After taking the poison, Socrates continued to talk with his friends. Gradually, his body grew cold and his eyes became fixed. With great sadness, his friends covered him after he died. In his dialogue *Phaedo*, Plato wrote, "Such was the end . . . of our comrade, who was, we may fairly say, of all those whom we knew in our time, the bravest and also the wisest and most upright man." [21]

Links to Plato

Socrates's life, his method of teaching, his wisdom in living, and his courage in dying inspired Plato to become a philosopher. In his youth, Plato had been active in politics, but after witnessing the democracy that put Socrates to his death, he withdrew from the political scene to concentrate on educating people through philosophy. Based on Socrates's ideas and way of life, Plato's own brilliant philosophy has become the foundation of all Western thought. Harvard philosopher Alfred North Whitehead once said, "All Western philosophy consists of a series of footnotes to Plato."

3

THE CLASSICAL PERIOD: PLATO

Plato is philosophy, and philosophy is Plato.
—Ralph Waldo Emerson

Plato considered Socrates his mentor. To show his admiration, he made Socrates the main character in his dialogues, a series of writing that included Socrates and other people engaged in philosophical conversations. In the dialogues, Socrates displayed the qualities of goodness and wisdom that Plato felt were the highest goals of human aspiration. Although Plato modeled his early philosophy after Socrates's teachings, his own philosophical thought has influenced thinkers around the world for more than 2,000 years.

CARING FOR THE SOUL

Before Plato, the pre-Socratics had asked questions about permanence and change in the universe. They wanted to know if there was a permanent substance that held together all that is changing. Deciding that we could never know the answer to those questions, the Sophists turned to rhetoric. Discouraged with the Sophists' beliefs that truth was unimportant, Socrates concentrated on living the good life by caring for the soul.

Plato's Life

Plato (427–347 B.C.) was born in Athens, Greece, when Socrates was about 42 years old. Athenian culture dominated the Western world, and Plato's family was one of the most distinguished families in Athens. His mother, Perictione, was a relative of the great Athenian lawmaker Solon. Plato's father, Ariston, who

Originally named Aristocles, Plato was a mathematician and Socrates's most renowned student. He established the Academy in Athens, the first institution of higher learning in the Western world, where he tutored another famous philosopher, the young Aristotle.

died when Plato was a child, traced his lineage to the old kings of Athens and to the god Poseidon. Plato's uncle Charmides and his cousin Critias were prominent aristocratic leaders. After his father's death, Plato's mother married her uncle Pyrilampes, who was one of the designers of Athenian democracy.

When Plato was a young man, Athens was fighting Sparta in the Peloponnesian Wars (431–404 B.C.). When Athens surrendered to Sparta, a group of powerful aristocrats known as "the Thirty" overthrew democracy and ruled Athens for three years. Plato's family was part of this group, and they asked Plato to join them, but Plato, disgusted by their unethical practices, refused the offer. Yet, the Thirty could not restore aristocratic rule, and soon democracy was reinstated. Plato again thought of going into politics but was repelled when two politicians, Anytus and Meletus, brought Socrates to trial on false charges, and a jury condemned Socrates to death. This injustice made such a deep impression on Plato that he left Athens. A just government, he said, would never have murdered a man such as the godlike Socrates.

After 12 years of travel and intense study, Plato returned to Athens where he established the Academy, the first university in the Western world. The school stood in a grove of trees that was once owned by a Greek hero named Academus. Plato headed the Academy and continued to write until he died at the age of 80. His most distinguished student at the Academy was Aristotle, who also became a famous philosopher.

Socrates's Method at Work

The Sophists believed that our minds are blank at birth and that our ideas of right or wrong come from the societies we live in. Therefore, these ideas will vary from one society to another. There is, they said, no such thing as eternal or universal principles for living the good life. Socrates and Plato strongly disagreed, arguing that true knowledge lies hidden within our souls, and through the dialectic method, the truth could be drawn out of a person. The dialectic method is important because it leads the mind beyond the changing physical world to unchanging eternal principles. Socrates and Plato argued that the mind knew the principles of Truth, Beauty, and Goodness in its preexistence, before its earthly existence.

The Soul

In his dialogue *The Republic*, Plato described the soul as having three parts (Figure 1). They are 1) the reason and intuition, or the rational; 2) the spirited, or nonrational; and 3) the appetites, or irrational. He arrived at this conclusion by analyzing the three kinds of activities going on in human beings. First, he analyzed the motivation for Goodness and Truth, controlled by the reason and intuition. Then, he analyzed the drive toward action, controlled by the spirited. Third, he analyzed the desire for pleasures of the body, controlled by the appetites.

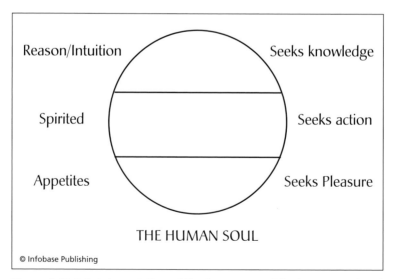

Reason/Intuition   Seeks knowledge

Spirited   Seeks action

Appetites   Seeks Pleasure

THE HUMAN SOUL

© Infobase Publishing

Figure 1. Plato's interpretation of the three parts of the human soul and the activities each controls.

The spirited is neutral and inclined to follow the rational intuition and reason, but because it is neutral, it can also be pulled toward the appetites.

Reason and intuition seek the true goal of human life by seeing things according to their true nature. The spirited and the appetites, however, desire worldly pleasures that can fool the reason and intuition into believing that pleasures of the senses (taste, touch, sight, hearing, and smell) will bring us happiness. The opposite is true, however. Unhappiness results when we think that physical pleasures are more important than the soul.

Immortality of the Soul

Plato believed that the soul preexists before it enters the body and that it will continue to exist after the body dies. His dialogue *Phaedo* records a conversation that Socrates had with his friend Cebes and others on the day of his death. They discuss the immortality of the soul.

> *Socrates:* And now, . . . if we are agreed that the immortal is imperishable, then the soul will be not immortal only, but also imperishable; otherwise we shall require another argument.
> *Cebes:* Nay, . . . there is no need of that, as far as this point goes; for if the immortal, which is eternal, will admit of destruction, what will not?
> *Socrates:* And all men would admit, . . . that God, and the essential form of life, and all else that is immortal, never perishes.
> *Cebes:* All men, indeed, . . . and, what is more, I think, all gods would admit that.
> *Socrates:* Then if the immortal is indestructible, must not the soul, if it be immortal, be imperishable?

Cebes: Certainly, it must.

Socrates: Then, it seems when death attacks a man, his mortal part dies, but his immortal part retreats before death, and goes away sage and indestructible.

Cebes: It seems so.

Socrates: Then, Cebes, beyond all question the soul is immortal and imperishable, and our souls will indeed exist in the other world. [22]

According to Plato, at the end of life the body dies, but the soul does not die because it is immortal. Each soul will pass through many lifetimes, and while in a body, it may seek knowledge or it may indulge in sensuous physical pleasures.

As a believer in reincarnation, Plato said that each soul is reborn according to what it deserves. If I am selfish, mean, and resentful in this life, then my soul must come into another life to learn how to overcome such negativity. If I am loyal, virtuous, and strive for knowledge in this life, my soul will reap the rewards of these positive characteristics in a next life. Our present life is based on our past thoughts and actions, and our future life will be a result of our present thoughts and actions. Thus, each soul chooses its future character and destiny according to what it needs to learn.

Moral Philosophy

Because our souls preexist in the eternal realm of Truth, Beauty, and Goodness, Plato believed that all people are basically good. Yet, soon after we are born, we become enticed by the world of pleasure. Such ignorance, however, is weaker than truth, and after several lifetimes our souls begin to awaken to the truth. This awakening stirs the soul with a yearning to return to its true home. Plato called this yearning "eros," or love. From the point of awakening, the material world becomes less important than striving for truth and the progress of the soul.

Theory of Knowledge

Plato contended there are two ways we can awaken out of ignorance into knowledge: through our own insight and awareness or with the help of a teacher or guide. In his famous "Allegory of the Cave," Plato relates a story illustrating the journey of the soul from ignorance to knowledge.

Allegory of the Cave

Plato asks us to imagine a group of people living in an underground cave. They sit with their backs to the opening of the cave, their arms and legs bound so they can see only what is in front of them—the shadows on the wall of the cave. Behind these people is a walkway on which humanlike creatures carry various animals, plants, and other objects. Behind the walkway is a fire that casts flickering shadows of the creatures and the objects on the wall of the cave. Surprisingly, the cave dwellers think the shadows on the wall are real objects because they have been looking only at the wall since they were born.

Someone then comes and unchains one of the cave dwellers, taking him back to the figures and fire. At first, the cave dweller would be shocked to see that the figures on the wall are more than just shadows. He would be frightened of this new discovery and want to turn back to his seat in the cave. Yet, said Plato, he cannot return to his seat because he continues to be led past the fire to the outside of the dark cave. The natural light would almost blind the cave dweller, but once he got accustomed to the beauty of seeing color and clear shapes, he would hesitate about going back to his old life in the dark cave. Then, he would see the Sun in the sky, and realize that the Sun, symbolizing God as the source of all things, is what gives life to these animals and flowers and everything else in the world.

The cave dweller, now free from the ignorance of the cave, rejoices in this newfound knowledge. Realizing the joy of discovering Truth, Beauty, and Goodness, he returns to the cave to set the other prisoners free. Once he returns to the darkness of the cave, however, he is unable to convince the others that the shadows on the wall are merely reflections of reality. In fact, when he tries to release them from their chains and help them out of the cave, they try to kill him.

Plato's "Allegory of the Cave" shows us the journey we must all make from the physical world that is ignorance, to the realm of eternal Truth, Beauty, and Goodness that is reality. Because they are ignorant, the people inside the cave are satisfied to live among the shadows, and they do not give much thought to what is causing the shadows. As the cave dweller had to turn completely around to see the light, the entire soul must turn away

This sixteenth-century colored engraving presents an unknown French artist's interpretation of Plato's "Allegory of the Cave." The allegory, which explains Plato's concept of the Forms as an answer to the problem of universals, appears in Plato's *Republic,* written in about 360 B.C.

from believing that the physical world of the senses is as important as the knowledge of Truth, Beauty, and Goodness. Plato knew that turning the soul around would not be easy. Even the "noblest natures," he said, do not want to look away from their routine lifestyles.

The Divided Line

Plato thought the physical world of change is a world of appearances, making it less real than the eternal truths. In his simile "The Divided Line" (Figure 2), he used a more systematic method to explain the stages we go through on our journey to knowledge. Plato thought that, to reach knowledge, the mind moves through four stages of development: 1) imaging, 2) belief, 3) thinking, and 4) reason/intuition. Each stage represents a different way of looking at the world and provides a basis for distinguishing between objects perceptible to our physical senses and objects in the intelligible world reached by thought. Reasoning/intuition gives us the broadest view of the world. Imaging gives us the most limited view of the world. In the simile, presented in his work *The Republic*, Plato uses Socrates to describe "The Divided Line" to Plato's brother Glaucon:

> "Well, take a line divided into two unequal parts, corresponding to the visible and intelligible worlds, and then divide the two parts again in the same ratio, to represent degrees of clarity and obscurity. In the visible world, one section stands for images: by 'images' I mean first shadows, then reflections in the water and other close grained polished surfaces, and all that sort of thing if you understand me."

> *"I understand."*

"Let the other section stand for the objects which are the originals of the images—animals, plants and manufactured objects of all kinds."

"Very good."

"Would you be prepared to admit that these sections differ in their degree of truth, and that the relation of image to the original is the same as that of opinion and knowledge?"

"I would."

"Then consider next how the intelligible part of the line is to be divided. In one section the mind uses the originals of the visible world in their turn as images, and has to base its inquiries on assumptions and proceed from them to its conclusions instead of going back to first principles: in the other it proceeds from assumption

A (Images)	B (Visible Things)	C (Mathematical Objects)	D (Forms)

Figure 2. A visual representation of Plato's Divided Line.

Objects	*y*	States of Mind	
	D	The Good (Forms)	Intelligence Reason/Intuition
World of Ideas			Knowledge
	C	Mathematical Objects	Thinking/ Reason
	B	Physical (Visible Things)	Belief (Opinion)
Physical World			Opinion
	A	Images	Imaging (Illusion)

x

© Infobase Publishing

Figure 3. This table corresponds to *Figure 2*. Here, the vertical line from *x* to *y* suggests that there is some degree of knowledge at each stage, from the lowest to the highest. The horizontal line that separates *A* and *B* from *C* and *D* separates the physical world from the world of ideas. The right side of the graph represents the mind, and the left side represents the objects that correspond to the mind on that level.

back to self-sufficient first principles, making no use of the images employed by the other section, but pursuing its inquiry solely by means of Forms. . . .

"It treats assumptions not as principles, but as assumptions in the true sense, that is, as starting points and steps in the ascent to the universal, self-sufficient first principle; when it has reached that principle it can again descend, by keeping to the consequences that follow from it, to a final conclusion. The whole procedure involves nothing in the sensible world, but deals throughout with Forms and finishes with Forms." [23]

Toward the end of the discussion between Glaucon and Socrates, Glaucon remarks that the process of climbing out of the shadows to enlightenment sounds like a long and tedious job. Socrates agrees, adding:

> And you may assume that there are, corresponding to the four sections of the line, four states of mind: to the top section Intelligence, to the second Reason [Thinking], to the third Opinion [Belief], and to the fourth Illusion [Imaging]. And you may arrange them in a scale, and assume that they have degrees of clarity corresponding to the degree of truth and reality possessed by their subject-matter. [24]

Imaging Stage

At the imaging stage, people look to others for answers because they have not learned to think for themselves. As the cave dwellers in "The Allegory of the Cave" believed that the shadows are real, those who are at the imaging stage believe that most of what they hear on TV and read in the newspaper is true. Advertisers address their audience at the imaging level. They want to convince us that buying a particular product will change our lives, make us happier, better looking, or more popular.

The imaging stage correlates to the shadows on the wall in Plato's allegory. Our shadow is no more the truth of our body than a postcard of Niagara Falls is of seeing it in person. Actually seeing physical objects raises us to the next level of knowledge— the belief stage.

Belief Stage

Plato used the words belief and opinion rather than knowledge to describe the physical world. Our senses tell us the physical world is real because we can see it and touch it. Experiencing objects directly with our eyes gives us more information than seeing shadows or pictures of them. For example, we often hear the statement, "Seeing is believing." Yet, seeing physical objects only tells us what the object looks like on the outside. Viewing Niagara Falls gives us a sense of its physical splendor but no information about its age, the origin of its formation, or the water that runs over it. Belief, just as imaging, is a matter of opinion. *I* can believe that Niagara Falls is the most beautiful sight in America, but *you* can argue that the Grand Canyon is the most beautiful. Our judgments are a matter of opinion. If, however, we decide to explore the scientific evidence that explains the cause and formation of Niagara Falls and the Grand Canyon, then we move from the belief stage to the thinking stage.

Thinking Stage

When we advance from belief to thinking, we proceed from the visible world of the senses to the invisible world of ideas. We now enter the world of knowledge. Plato believed that scientists were the bridge builders between the two worlds— opinion and knowledge—because science forces us to think about the principles and laws behind physical objects. When geologists study Niagara Falls, they think about the water source and origin of the rock formations, not about a picture postcard of the falls.

In the thinking stage, we think of the "idea human," whether we see short, tall, dark, light, young, or old people. Thinking gives us more knowledge than belief or imaging because it takes us beyond the physical body to human characteristics, such as moral values. Although thinking gives us some knowledge, it has limitations. Thinking knows that two plus two always equals four, but it does not know why. Likewise, thinking knows people are good or bad, but it does not know why. Plato said that thinking alone cannot take us to the highest level of knowledge because thinking cannot answer the *why* questions in life.

Intelligence (Reason/Intuition) Stage

At the highest stage of knowledge, the mind deals directly with the Forms. For Plato, Forms are eternal ideas beyond the physical world. Forms do not apply to the physical world because they are in a realm beyond time and space. We cannot experience Forms with our five senses because Forms have no size, shape, color, or weight. Because objects in the physical world will erode over time, Plato said the physical world is not the true reality. It is only a world of appearance. Forms, however, are the true reality: They are the eternal patterns, or blueprints, of everything in the world.

Plato said there are many Forms, such as Human, Dog, or Tree. For example, examine the Form Dog. All dog species look different. Some are poodles, others dalmatians, and still others collies or mutts. They may be spotted, tall or short, fat or thin. Yet, despite their many differences, dogs share one thing in common: the eternal Form Dog. The Form Dog that makes it possible for us to recognize all of them as dogs.

Plato said there are three ways to know the Forms. They are through remembering, by using the dialectic method, and through love. To Plato, developing the proper kind of love is as difficult as cultivating our intelligence.

The Ladder of Love

For Plato, love merges with beauty, and in his dialogue the *Symposium*, he guides us through the stages of love to the soul's immortality. At the first and lowest stage of the Ladder of Love, we fall in love with the beauty of a physical body. In short, this is a chemical attraction. Second, we love the beauty of art, nature, and the physical world. Third, we move to the love of a friend, called "Platonic love," and fourth, to the love of institutions, such as schools and other institutions that better the world. Fifth, we discover our love of learning about the universe. From this love of learning we move to the sixth and final stage, Plato's "wondrous vision" of the Form Beauty itself and its everlasting loveliness for which the soul has always yearned. At this point in our awareness, we will understand that every lovely thing in the physical world and in the soul shares in the Form Beauty, and this joyful experience makes life worth living.

Plato's Symposium, painted by Anselm Feuerbach in 1869, depicts one of Plato's most celebrated philosophical dialogues. Plato's work is a discussion on the nature of love, presented in a series of satiric and serious speeches given by a group of characters, including Socrates, the central figure in Plato's numerous dialogues.

In Plato's *Symposium*, Socrates recalls to his friends the words of his teacher, Diotima, whom Plato calls his "instructress in the art of love":

> Starting from individual beauties, the quest for the universal beauty must find him ever mounting the heavenly ladder, stepping from rung to rung—that is, from one to two, and from two to *every* lovely body, from bodily beauty to the beauty of institutions, from institutions to learning, and from learning in general to the special lore that pertains to nothing but the beautiful itself—until at last he comes to know what beauty is.
>
> And now, Socrates, there bursts upon him that wondrous vision which is the very soul of the beauty he has toiled so long for. It is an everlasting loveliness which neither comes nor goes. . . .
>
> And if, my dear Socrates, Diotima went on, man's life is ever worth the living, it is when he has attained this vision of the very soul of beauty. [25]

Political Philosophy and the Ideal State

In *Republic*, we find the first examples of utopian literature in the Western world. The dialogue begins with Socrates and some friends gathered to discuss the meaning of justice. They decide to find the meaning of justice by constructing the "ideal state," or the best possible form of government (Figure 4). They agree to base the ideal state on the human soul's three parts: reason and intuition, the spirited, and the appetites.

They first decide that a society must have people who can produce food, shelter, and clothing, such as farmers, builders, and weavers. These craftsmen belong to the artisan class. The artisans supply the material goods of the state and are lovers of pleasure,

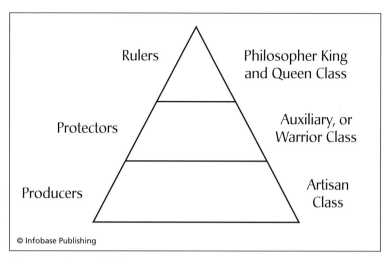

Figure 4. Plato's Ideal State.

represented by the appetites. To control the internal state of affairs and the defense of the state, an auxiliary, or warrior class, is necessary. These men and women defend the state and are ruled by the spirited aspect of the soul. Finally, the state needs rulers—a philosopher king and queen class. Ruled by the rational part of the soul, these individuals will make laws and govern the state wisely. Because they strive for Truth, Beauty, and Goodness, the philosopher kings and queens want what is good for the state.

Each class has particular duties, and like the soul, each class has certain limitations. As seekers of worldly pleasures, the artisan class is the only one to have money and own private property. These people may marry and have families. Because most people enjoy worldly pleasures, this will be the largest class. Yet, they have no voice about the laws of the land or its defense. The warrior class defends the state. They live in communities, and they may not marry, handle money, or own private property. Plato argued that, the warriors should be free from the bonds of material possessions, and, therefore, would hold property and families collectively rather than individually. Plato argued that, if the entire warrior class was a single family, its members would have fewer temptations to acquire money and possessions. Sexual relations would occur at special festivals. At birth, children would be given into the care of nurses, so each warrior would treat each child with love and respect. The warrior class must obey the rules of the philosopher king and queen class.

The philosopher king and queen class is at the highest level in the ideal state. As wise rulers, they will show kindness and justice to all. They may own nothing and would live a simple life supported by the state. Through a special breeding program, the philosopher kings and queens will bear children who hopefully will be future rulers of the ideal state. Anyone reaching the philosopher king and queen class will have had at least 30 years of education. Therefore, not all citizens would be eligible to be part of this class.

Plato believed that only philosophers should rule. He considered democracy a lower form of government because in a democracy people vote for the most popular candidate who promises the most to the appetites of the masses. Also, this kind of candidate would not be the best ruler because he or she would make the rational part of the soul a slave to the appetites and spirited parts. Finally, it was a democracy that put Socrates, Plato's inspiration, to death. Justice in the ideal state, therefore, reflects the good individual and the reason and intuition that rules the spirited and appetites.

Links to Aristotle

Plato's notions of the Forms, the ideal state, and justice had a profound impact on his students. Aristotle, Plato's student at the Academy, was deeply influenced by his teacher. Although Aristotle departed from some of Plato's ideas, he praised Plato as a wise philosopher and noble man. Despite his devotion to his teacher, Aristotle went on to establish his own philosophical teachings, very unique from Plato's.

4

THE CLASSICAL PERIOD: ARISTOTLE

All men by nature desire knowledge.
—Aristotle

Aristotle's influence in the Western world was so profound that, for hundreds of years after his death, he was known simply as The Philosopher. Aristotle came to Plato's Academy when he was 17 years old and was considered Plato's most gifted student. Many of today's philosophers consider Aristotle the greatest philosopher who ever lived.

While Plato focused on the timeless and spaceless world of eternal Forms to find reality, Aristotle got down on his hands and knees to study the natural world of plants and animals as well as human beings. Plato, the metaphysician, someone who speculates on things beyond the physical world, loved the abstract world of Truth, Beauty, and Goodness. Aristotle, the scientist and logician, loved to study nature and our role in it. Both philosophers wanted to discover what is real. Both agreed that there are Forms, but they disagreed on their meaning. As we have seen, Plato found reality in the eternal world of Forms and considered the physical world of change an appearance or reflection of reality but not reality itself. Aristotle, however, placed greater value on the physical world by suggesting that the Forms were united with it.

Although Aristotle turned much of his attention to the physical world of nature, he thought the pre-Socratic answers for the substances that constitute reality—water, air, the boundless, seeds, and atoms—were limited. Aristotle believed that those thinkers had not provided significant accounts of human qualities, especially morality. Like Plato, Aristotle asked the question, "What is the good life?" The answer he developed gave birth to a completely new view of morality.

Aristotle's Life

Aristotle (384–322 B.C.) was born in Stagira, a Greek town on the northeast coast of Thrace. His mother came from a family of physicians, and his father was the doctor to the king of Macedonia, a region in northern Greece. When Aristotle was 17, his parents sent him to Plato's Academy where he remained for 20 years, first as a student and later as a lecturer. At the Academy, Aristotle was known as The Mind of the School.

Plato's genius and noble character had a deep influence on Aristotle, and no matter what their differences were philosophically, Aristotle admired Plato all of his life. After Plato's death, Aristotle left the Academy to write and teach. He married, but his wife died giving birth to their daughter. Later, Aristotle met Herpyllis with whom he had a long and happy relationship. He dedicated his book on moral philosophy, *Nicomachean Ethics*, to their son, Nicomachus.

When Aristotle was 40, King Philip of Macedonia asked him to tutor his 13-year-old son, Alexander, who would later be known as Alexander the Great. As Alexander grew up, he and Aristotle became good friends, but they disagreed on what was the best type of government. Aristotle thought that a government should be no larger than the city-state, but Alexander envisioned a world empire. Also, Aristotle thought that Greeks were superior to all other races, while Alexander believed that all races were equal

Aristotle was a student of Plato and later taught Alexander the Great. He wrote on many subjects, such as poetry, theater, biology, zoology, politics, government, rhetoric, ethics, and logic.

and should be integrated. Their friendship survived such differences, however, and Alexander, while away in foreign lands, often sent Aristotle samples of rare flora and fauna for scientific study.

In 336 B.C., when Alexander was 20 years old, his father was murdered. Alexander became king. A year later, Aristotle founded a school in Athens, the Lyceum. There, Aristotle and his students strolled under tree-covered walks discussing science and philosophy. The specimens that Alexander had sent, along with his collection of maps and manuscripts, helped Aristotle form the first important library in the Western world. A master of many subjects, Aristotle invented logic, or laws of thought, and wrote treatises on physics, biology, ethics, meteorology, metaphysics, political science, and poetics.

While Aristotle was teaching science and philosophy at the Lyceum, Alexander was changing the world. By the time he was 30 years old, Alexander ruled Greece, Persia, Egypt, and Asia. When Alexander died in 323 B.C., a wave of anti-Macedonian feeling swept Athens, and many Athenians expressed hostility toward Aristotle for having been Alexander's friend. Recalling Socrates's fate, Aristotle left Athens and the Lyceum, "lest the Athenians should sin twice against philosophy." He settled on the island of Euboea, his mother's birthplace, where he died a year later of a stomach illness.

Form and Matter

Like Plato and the philosophers before him, Aristotle also wanted to know what is real. The pre-Socratics had searched for reality in the material universe. Plato, the metaphysician, had found reality in the Forms, the eternal and perfect ideas. As a scientist, Aristotle took a different view. He agreed with Plato that the form (not capitalized for Aristotle) horse is eternal, but he said we could not know the form horse if it existed in a realm beyond the physical world because we cannot know that realm. To know the form horse, we must see an actual physical horse, because the form, or characteristics, of a horse are in the horse itself. The same is true of matter. To know the substance matter, we must see an actual physical object, such as the horse. For Aristotle, form and matter must come together in the same object before we can know them. "There is no form without matter and no matter without form," he said. We can only know the forms by studying the physical objects in the world because all things, including humans, are a combination of matter and form.

Potentiality and Actuality

Matter is the substance out of which everything in the world is made, and form is the thing's essence, or its characteristics. Matter contains the potentiality to realize a specific form, which is its actuality. For example, the newborn human has the potentiality to become an adult human being, its actuality. The acorn has the potentiality to become an oak tree. Everything in nature has a built-in potentiality to realize its purpose or actuality. Aristotle argued that nature's built-in form assures that humans will always be humans and never fish, that oak trees will always be oak trees and never turnips, and that horses will always be horses and never kangaroos.

The Four Causes

Aristotle discovered four causes that govern change in everything from art to nature as they develop from their potentiality to their actuality. The four causes are: 1) the formal cause; or form; 2) the material cause, or matter; 3) the efficient cause, or motion; and 4) the final cause, or end.

In carving a marble statue, the formal cause is the plan the sculptor has in mind, the material cause is the marble, the efficient cause is the sculptor shaping the statue, and the final cause is the end, or purpose of the statue, which would be as a decoration. For Aristotle, everything in nature contains these four causes and the potential to grow into its actuality. Everything in nature is always in motion, eternally moving and changing. What keeps everything in motion is the Unmoved Mover.

The Unmoved Mover

Just as everything in nature has the potential to strive for its actuality, or end, there is something beyond nature, something that is pure actuality—the final cause. Pure actuality, said Aristotle, is eternal, immaterial, and perfect because it has no potentiality. He called pure actuality the "Unmoved Mover," another term for God or the principle of eternal motion.

Because motion is eternal, there never was a time when the world did not exist. Therefore, the Unmoved Mover is not a creator god. Being pure actuality, it has no physical body, and, lacking nothing, it has no emotional desires. The activity of the Unmoved Mover consists of pure thought. As pure thought, the Unmoved Mover thinks only perfection, which is itself.

Recall that for Aristotle, all creatures in nature, including human beings, strive to realize their actuality. Because the highest human faculty is reason, we find our perfection in contemplating the Unmoved Mover. Being perfect in everything, including love, the Unmoved Mover's perfect love attracts our thoughts to it.

> The . . . [Unmoved Mover] then moves things because it is loved, whereas all other things move because they are themselves moved. . . . But since there is something that moves things, while being itself immovable and existing in actuality, it is not possible in any way for that thing to be in any state other than that in which it is. . . . The first mover, then, must exist, and insofar as he exists of necessity, his existence must be good; and thus he must be a first principle. . . .
>
> It is upon a principle of this kind, then, that the heavens and nature depend. [26]

Love is motion, even as Empedocles and Plato claimed, and the Unmoved Mover is the "Form of the world" moving it toward its divine end, its actuality. The highest activity of human reason is not unlike the activity of the Unmoved Mover, except the Unmoved Mover thinks only perfection, and we can only think *about* perfection. Being imperfect, we do not have the ability to think perfection itself, yet the happiest life for us is thinking about the Unmoved Mover.

The Soul

Plato believed that the soul was separate from the body, but for Aristotle, the soul could not function without the body, nor could the body exist without the soul. He argued there could be no soul without the body any more than there could be vision without an eye. The soul is the form, or the actuality, of the body, claims Aristotle:

> What is soul? . . .
>
> Among substances are by general consent reckoned bodies and especially natural bodies; for they are the principles of all other bodies. Of natural bodies some have life in them, others not; by life we mean self-nutrition and growth (with its correlative decay). It follows that every natural body which has life in it is a substance in the sense of a composite.
>
> But since it is also a *body* of such and such a kind, viz. having life, the *body* cannot be soul, the body is the subject or matter, not what is attributed to. Hence the soul must be a substance in the sense of the form of a natural body having life potentially within it. But substance is actuality, and thus soul is the actuality [form] of a body. [27]

By separating the soul and body, Plato spoke of the soul's preexistence and immortality. Furthermore, Plato argued that gaining knowledge was the process of remembering what the soul knew in its preexistent state. Aristotle disagreed. Aristotle argued that, without the body, the soul cannot exist, and without the soul, the body can't exist. When a human baby is born into the world, its mind is like a blank sheet of paper. The soul comes into existence with the body, and with the death of the body, the soul also perishes.

> Mind is in a sense potentially whatever is thinkable, though actually it is nothing until it has thought. What it thinks must be in it just as characters may be said to be on a writing-tablet on which as yet nothing actually stands written: this is exactly what happens with mind. [28]

Aristotle was born in the ancient Greek city of Stagira, Thrace, at the northern end of the Aegean Sea in 384 B.C. These pure gold objects were found by three factory workers in Thrace in 1949 and date back to the turn of the fourth and third centuries B.C.

For Aristotle, there are three types of souls that make up the human body. They are:

1) the nutritive; 2) the sensitive; and 3) the rational. The nutritive part of the soul has life; it is present in plants, as well as in the human body. The sensitive part of the soul has both nutritive and the sensitive (our five senses), and is also present in animals. The human soul, however, contains all three types of souls because the rational, our ability to reason, is unique to the human being. That is why Aristotle called humans "rational animals."

The Senses

Sense experience is more important to Aristotle than to Plato. Plato said our highest type of reasoning and intuition goes beyond sense experience. Aristotle believed that reason and the senses work together. The eye, for example, sees a yellow rose, and with reason, we can analyze and understand the contents of the yellow rose. Without seeing the yellow rose, the mind would have no concept of it.

Human reason, said Aristotle, is both passive and active. The passive mind, our sense mind, is a blank tablet on which our senses write. Because the passive mind depends on our senses to function, this aspect of the soul is not eternal. The active mind, our reason, is eternal because it is similar to the mind of the Unmoved Mover. At the death of the body, the passive mind, the senses, and the nutritive part of the soul all die. Yet, because the active mind exists eternally whether we exist or not, there is no personal immortality.

Moral Philosophy

Aristotle's moral philosophy was the outcome of his metaphysics. He believed that everything in nature aims at some "end": its actuality. Because the end is the fulfillment of each thing's function, Aristotle called it "good." The end of the acorn is the oak tree. The end of making money is wealth:

> Every art and every inquiry, and similarly every action and choice, is thought to aim at some good; and for this reason the good has rightly been declared to be that at which all things aim. . . . Now, as there are many actions, arts, and sciences, their ends also are many; the end of the medical art is health, that of shipbuilding a vessel, that of strategy victory, that of economics wealth. [29]

To find the purpose of human morality, Aristotle asked, "What is the 'good' at which humans aim?" Plato had thought that the highest human good was to soar beyond the senses to the world of ideas, to know the Form of the Good. If we knew the Good, then we would do the good. Yet, Aristotle argued that the good is for everything to realize its own true nature. The good is within things. So, what is the good at which all humans aim? Aristotle's answer is "happiness."

> The good we are seeking . . . [is] surely that for whose sake everything else is done. In medicine this is health, in strategy victory, in architecture a house. . . .
>
> Since there are evidently more than one end, and we choose some of these (e.g. wealth, flutes, and in general instruments) for the sake of something else, clearly not all ends are complete ends: but the chief good is evidently something complete. Therefore, if there is only one complete end, this will be what we are seeking. . . . Now we call that which is in itself worthy of pursuit more complete than that which is worthy of pursuit for the sake of something else, and that which is never desirable for the sake of something else more complete than the things

that are desirable both in themselves and for the sake of that other thing, and therefore we call complete without qualification that which is always desirable in itself and never for the sake of something else.

This 1665 painting by noted French artist Charles LeBrun shows Alexander the Great riding in a chariot as he enters the city of Babylon after its fall to the young conqueror in 331 B.C.

Now such a thing happiness, above all else, is held to be; for this we choose always for itself and never for the sake of something else, but honour, pleasure, reason, and every excellence we choose indeed for themselves . . . but we choose them also for the sake of happiness, judging that through them we shall be happy. Happiness, on the other hand, no one chooses for the sake of these, nor, in general, for anything other than itself. . . .

Happiness, then, is something complete and self-sufficient, and is the end of action. [30]

If happiness is the good at which all people aim, then why are people often unhappy? If we were only rational, said Aristotle, we would be virtuous and, thus, happy. Yet, the irrational nutritive and sensitive parts of the soul often conflict with the reason. This conflict raises the problem of morality. Suppose you are in a department store looking for a present for your mother. You see a pair of earrings that she would like. There is no salesperson to help you and no shoppers in the jewelry department. The irrational part of you wants to slip the earrings into your pocket. The rational part of you warns that stealing is wrong. This kind of conflict raises the problem of morality. In this scenario, what is the right, or moral, choice to make? Aristotle said it takes practice to be moral. The happy person is not one who does a good deed now and then but the person whose whole life is good.

The Golden Mean

For Aristotle, virtue, or moral goodness, is a mean between two extremes, which he called "vices" (Figure 5). For example, Aristotle advised that we must not have too much fear or too little fear. Instead, we must have courage—the mean between two extremes. If we fear everything, we are cowardly. If we rush to meet every danger, we are rash. Likewise, we must have neither too much pride nor poor self-esteem. Instead, we must have self-respect, a mean between the vices of too much pride and poor self-esteem. Balance, or finding our mean, said Aristotle, is the key to happiness.

Because our individual characters and circumstances vary, the mean is different for each person. The mean of generosity is far different for a wealthy person than for a struggling factory worker. There will be a contrast in the mean of modesty between the naturally shy introvert and the naturally outgoing extrovert. Each of us must find our mean between two extremes. However, Aristotle said some actions such as spite, envy, jealousy, adultery, murder, and theft have no mean at all. To do them under any conditions is simply wrong.

Excess (Vice)	Mean (Virtue)	Defect (Vice)
Foolhardy	Courageous	Cowardly
Gluttony	Moderation	Starvation
Wasteful	Generosity	Stingy
Vanity	Pride	Too humble
Buffoonery	Humor	Boorish
Too shy	Modesty	Shows off

© Infobase Publishing

Figure 5. Examples of Aristotle's Virtue of the Golden Mean. Good judgment requires that we find the mean, or virtue, between the vices of excess and defect.

Political Philosophy

"Man is by nature a political animal," said Aristotle. He meant that living in a community and developing a form of government is a natural function of human beings. Aristotle thought there were three good forms of government. The best government is monarchy, or one with a king as the sole ruler; the second-best form of government is aristocracy with a few rulers; and the most practical government is polity with many rulers.

For a monarchy to be effective, the king must govern for the good of the people rather than being a selfish tyrant. For an aristocracy to work well, it, too, must be careful not to degenerate into a government that is run by a few tyrants. Polity, the third form of government, must not degenerate into a democracy, which could develop into mob rule, according to Aristotle. For any form of government to succeed, the state must be sure that no class of people has too much money or too little money, for in politics, as in daily life, extremes breed immorality.

Links to Hellenistic Philosophy

Since the time of Aristotle, philosophy of the Western world has generally been divided into two camps—the Platonic and the Aristotelian. Although most Westerners throughout history have turned to Aristotle's scientific view of the world as real and knowable, the writings of Plato also deeply influenced all subsequent philosophy. Thinkers in the next great age of philosophy, the Hellenistic period, took the philosophies of Plato and Aristotle and combined them with those of Socrates to fashion a new wave of Western thought.

5

THE HELLENISTIC PERIOD

There is nothing to fear but fear itself.
—Epictetus

After Aristotle's death in 322 B.C., and the death of his student Alexander the Great in 323 B.C., a new era in philosophical thought began—the Hellenistic period. Hellenistic philosophy covers approximately a 300-year period in Greek history, extending from the conquests of Alexander the Great to the conquering of his kingdoms by the Romans. The term *Hellenism* refers to both the time period and the Greek culture that flourished in the kingdoms of Macedonia, Syria, and Egypt.

Alexander's armies had marched across Greece, Egypt, Persia (present-day Iran), Afghanistan, and Pakistan, all the way to the Indus River. His victories linked Egypt and the Orient to the Greek civilization for the first time in history. In approximately A.D. 50, however, Rome declared war on the Hellenistic kingdoms, defeated the Greeks, and became the West's new superpower. Soon after conquering the Hellenistic regions, Roman politics and the Latin language spread from Spain to Asia.

As countries and cultures merged, religious beliefs and philosophy began to change. Asian religion mingled with Greek beliefs, giving birth to new religious ideas. When cultures and city-states broke down, people experienced doubt and anxiety about their religions and philosophies of life. These uncertainties brought with them a wave of pessimism that spread throughout many lands.

Generally, people were less interested in the universe and theories of human nature than they were with their own individual lives. Thus, Hellenistic philosophers tended to concentrate on practical everyday concerns about life and death. They looked to giants such as Socrates, Plato, and Aristotle as the source of their inspiration. Scientific ideas also shifted from one culture to another. Although Athens remained the center of philosophy, Alexandria, a city on the Nile River Delta in Egypt, became the new center for science. Intellectuals flocked to Alexandria because it had the best library in the ancient Western world and a fine museum dedicated to scientific studies.

The upheavals in the Hellenistic world were similar to the challenges we face today. Toward the end of the twentieth century, new ways of looking at philosophy, religion, and science spread throughout the Western world. A holistic view of our relationship to the planet and its creatures marked the beginning of a new epoch in these fields. In fact, much of our new thinking can actually be traced back to Hellenistic schools of thought. The ancients labored with the moral problems raised by Socrates, Plato, and Aristotle, asking, "How should we best live and die, and how do we achieve true happiness?" In the twenty-first century, we continue to ask similar questions, such as, "What is the meaning of life?" "How is everything interrelated?" "How should I live?" "Is there a God?" and, "What happens after we die?"

HELLENISTIC PHILOSOPHY

Five schools of philosophy shaped the ideas of the Hellenistic world: the Cynics, the Epicureans, the Stoics, the Skeptics, and the Neoplatonists. These groups of philosophers believed that only by understanding the nature of things could we find satisfactory answers to moral questions. They believed that our conduct depends on the kind of universe in which we live.

Most of these schools of philosophy based their theories on the metaphysical and ethical systems of Socrates, Plato, and Aristotle. The Cynics agreed with Socrates that material wealth and possessions are unimportant. The Epicureans, sometimes called "hedonists," believed that pleasure is good and pain is evil. They added, however, that overindulgence of any pleasure leads to pain. Therefore, true pleasure is living a calm, serene life. The Stoics, inspired by Socrates's courage in death, said the only way to achieve happiness is to control our emotional responses to events we could not change. The Skeptics doubted anything without proof. They followed Socrates's method of defining their terms and examining ideas. Plotinus, who founded Neoplatonism, looked to Plato for many of his metaphysical and moral ideas. He agreed with Plato that individual freedom depends on returning to our source through a mystical union with God.

The Cynic School

Once a student of Socrates, Antisthenes (c. 444–c. 365 B.C.) founded the Cynic school of philosophy in Athens. He agreed with Socrates that happiness has nothing to do with wealth, fame, or worldly success. Antisthenes said if we try to find happiness in worldly possessions, we will always be disappointed because no matter how much we have, we always want more. Not everyone can afford physical luxuries, he said, but everyone can find happiness, and once we find it, we never lose it.

The most famous of the Cynics, Diogenes (c. 404–323 B.C.), supposedly lived in a barrel. His only possessions were a tunic, a stick, and a little leather bag that he used to beg for food. The

Diogenes is considered one of the principal founders of the Cynic school of philosophy. A beggar living in the streets of Athens, he avoided earthly pleasure and believed that morality was shown by a return to the simplicities of nature.

description of Diogenes as a cynic is where the use of the word originates. *Cynic* is a Greek word meaning "dog." It was used to describe Diogenes because in rejecting all conventions of dress, food, and housing, he lived like a dog.

There is a story that tells of Diogenes sitting next to his barrel enjoying the warmth of the shining Sun. Alexander the Great rode up to Diogenes on his magnificent white horse. Impressed with Diogenes's reputation as a philosopher, Alexander asked if there was anything he could do for him. "Yes," said Diogenes. "Stand to one side, you are blocking the Sun." Another story tells that Diogenes was seen begging for food from a marble statue. When asked why, he answered, "So I'll get used to being refused."

Diogenes and the Cynic philosophers believed we should not become too emotionally involved in our health, our suffering, or even the thought of dying. Diogenes said there is nothing after death, so we have no reason to be afraid.

The Epicurean School

Epicurus (341–270 B.C.) founded the Epicurean school of philosophy in Athens, where he and his students would meet in a garden. Above the entrance to the school hung a sign that read, "Stranger, here you will live well. Here pleasure is the highest good." Greatly admired as a teacher, Epicurus was modest and friendly to everyone, including rich and poor, men and women, and even slaves.

Pleasure

Epicurus believed that pleasure is the highest good. Though the term *hedonism* has been attributed to his school, Epicurus himself ate plain foods and lived simply. Before taking a trip, a friend once asked Epicurus, "My revered teacher, what may I send you?" Epicurus replied, "Send me a cheese that I may fare sumptuously." He did not promote a hedonistic pleasure of gourmet foods or living a wild social life. True pleasure comes from living a simple life marked by a healthy body and soul. Gourmet foods upset the stomach, and too much social activity causes stress. Such sensuous pleasures, Epicurus argued, are shallow and unsatisfying.

> We consider that of desires some are natural, others vain, and of the natural some are necessary and others merely natural; and of the necessary some are necessary for happiness, others for the repose of the body, and others for choice and avoidance to the health of the body and freedom from disturbance, since this is the aim of the life of blessedness. For it is to obtain this end that we always act, namely, to avoid pain and fear. . . .
>
> And for this cause we call pleasure the beginning and end of the blessed life. For we recognize pleasure as the first good innate in us, and from pleasure we begin every act of choice and avoidance, and to pleasure we return again, using the feeling as the standard by which we judge every good. [31]

For Epicurus, some pleasures are intense and last for only a short time, such as going on a shopping spree. Other pleasures, such as acting morally, give us a sense of well-being. Because he insisted on living honorably and justly, Epicurus avoided politics and involvement in social affairs.

Afterlife

When asked about God and the afterlife, Epicurus said, "We must overcome the fear of the gods and the fear of death." Epicurus believed there is no life after death. For Epicurus, when we die, the body and soul disperse in all directions, and our personalities simply cease to be. Because "death is nothing to us," he claims, we should make life enjoyable. Wishing for immortality is foolish.

The Good Life

What makes life pleasurable? For Epicurus, happiness does not involve service to other people, helping suffering animals, or protecting the environment. The good life is the company of pleasant companions and studying philosophy. He believed that intellectual pleasures are always superior to bodily pleasures because they last longer and are free of pain.

The Stoic School

Like the Cynics and Epicureans, the Stoics recommended moderation of desires. The Cynics emphasized that we cannot find true happiness in material possessions. The Epicureans lived a life of simple intellectual and physical pleasures. The Stoics wanted a serene and controlled life through self-discipline.

Zeno

Zeno (334–262 B.C.) was the founder of the Stoic school of philosophy. He and his followers discussed and studied on the porch of his home. The name Stoic comes from the Greek word *stoa,* meaning "porch." Thus, Zeno and his followers were called "porch sitters." Stoicism has had a lasting influence on the Western world. We find Stoicism in Christianity and in the work of William Shakespeare. Today, we see elements of Stoicism in Jungian psychology and in therapy groups. Reinhold Niebuhr's "Serenity Prayer," used in Alcoholics Anonymous, was a prayer probably influenced by Stoic philosophy. It reads, "God, grant me the serenity to accept the things I cannot change, the courage to change the things I can, and the wisdom to know the difference."

God

Like the pre-Socratic Heraclitus, the Stoics viewed God as divine fire or Logos, the intelligence in all things. God is the divine fire that provides the universe with beauty, life, and order. Because everything has its source in God, God's reason governs the universe. This view is known as pantheism, the belief that God is in all and all is in God. Everything in the universe has the divine spark. God or Logos is natural law, and the same divine laws that govern nature determine human fate. In other words, whatever happens, happens for a reason. Nothing happens by chance.

Human Nature

For the Stoics, we humans are like microcosms reflecting the universal macrocosm. In other words, we are each a miniature universe. Each of us has the divine reason and a spark of the divine will. As God is the soul of the world, the human soul is part of God, and that is what gives us the ability to reason. Reason gives us the ability to understand the structure of the universe. In an orderly universe, nothing happens by chance. Therefore, we can only be happy by accepting our destiny. Some people are destined to play big parts, such as president of the United States, and others are destined to play minor parts. Nevertheless, whatever part we are destined to play is necessary in the overall scheme of things, and we must learn to play our part well.

Unlike the Epicureans, the Stoics did not look for the good in pleasure. Instead, they agreed with Socrates who identified the good with knowledge. The way to knowledge of the good is by controlling our emotions so they do not confuse the reason. We must learn to accept, with serenity, the things we cannot change. Freedom lies in our ability to change our attitude. Although we cannot change events that happen to us, we can change our attitude toward those events. The attitude we choose can make us happy or miserable. Wisdom, said the

Stoics, consists in our ability to recognize what is in our power and what is not in our power. External things such as the lives of our friends and growing old are not in our power. Our intentions, desires, and choices, however, are in our power.

Epictetus

Epictetus (c. A.D. 50–130) was born a slave in Phrygia, Asia Minor (present-day Turkey), but studied with a Stoic philosopher at Emperor Nero's court in Rome. While Epictetus was a slave, Nero had him tied to the stretching rack and tortured for teaching Stoic philosophy. In a story about his punishment, Epictetus says to the person in charge of the stretching rack, "If you turn the rack one more time both of my legs will break." When the rack was turned again and his legs snapped, Epictetus said calmly, "You see." Epictetus's calm acceptance of the things he could not change is the hallmark of the Stoic philosophy. For the rest of his life, Epictetus was lame.

After Nero's death in A.D. 68, Epictetus gained his freedom and began to teach. In A.D. 93, however, the new Roman emperor, Domitian, banished all philosophers from Rome. Epictetus went to northwestern Greece to establish a school of Stoicism and remained there for the rest of his life. He lived simply with only a mat, a pallet, and a clay lamp. Known for his kindness and humility, he married late in life to raise a baby whose parents were going to kill it by exposing the newborn to the elements.

The Right Attitude   Like Socrates, Epictetus wrote nothing, but one of his students, Flavius Arrianus, compiled notes that became the famous *Encheiridion*, or *Manual of Epictetus*. These notes illustrate the Stoic conviction that we cannot change events that happen to us. We can only change our attitude toward those events.

1. Some things are under our control, while others are
    not under our control. Under our control are concep-
    tion, choice, desire, aversion, and in a word, everything
    that is our own doing; not under our control are our

The Greek Stoic philosopher Epictetus believed that our ability to be
happy is dependent wholly on our own characters, how we relate to
ourselves, to others, and to the events in our lives. The ills we suffer,
says Epictetus, come from our mistaken beliefs about what is truly good.

body, our property, reputation, office and, in a word, everything that is not our own doing. Furthermore, the things under our control are by nature free, unhindered, and unimpeded; while the things not under our control are weak, servile, subject to hindrance, and not our own. Remember, therefore, that if what is naturally slavish you think to be free, and what is not your own to be your own, you will be hampered, will grieve, will be in turmoil, and will blame both gods and men; while if you think only what is your own to be your own, and what is not your own to be, as it really is, not your own, then no one will ever be able to exert compulsion upon you, no one will hinder you, you will blame no one, will find fault with no one, will do absolutely nothing against your will, you will have no personal enemy, no one will harm you, for neither is there any harm that can touch you. . . .

8. Do not seek to have everything that happens happen as you wish, but wish for everything to happen as it actually does happen, and your life will be serene. [32]

Fear　To live a meaningful life, we must overcome fear. "There is nothing to fear but fear itself," said Epictetus. If we learn to control our fears and our desires, serenity will follow. Epictetus reminded us that there is no need to fear the future or even death because they are going to happen in any case.

Marcus Aurelius

Marcus Aurelius (A.D. 121–180) was an emperor of Rome, revered by the people for his virtue, kindness, and wisdom. He showed concern for slaves and the poor and worked to correct the abuses in the jurisprudence system through legal reforms. Although he was a peace-loving man who enjoyed philosophy and literature, his role as emperor and general of the Roman Army cast him into politics and war. He and his wife had five sons, but only one of the five lived. On an expedition to the East, Aurelius's wife died. While on numerous military campaigns, he wrote privately, in a diary. These writings, which became known as *The Meditations*, were written for himself, not for teaching others. His words reflect his doubts and indecisions as well as his faith and his philosophy. In them, we can feel his pain and exhaustion along with his Stoic attitude toward his fate as emperor. After long and lonely years fighting one campaign after another, this Stoic warrior and saint died of smallpox at age 59.

View of the Universe　In *The Meditations*, Aurelius also wrote about his view of the universe. Like Heraclitus, he saw the world and everything in it in a state of flux. The universe, he said, is rational, and is made up of the divine soul. Humans share in the life and divinity of the universe, and each of us contains the divine spark. Life, Aurelius argued, is both beautiful and ugly, yet if we understand human nature, we can never be harmed.

> Say to yourself in the morning: I shall meet people who are interfering, ungracious, insolent, full of guile, deceitful and antisocial; they have all become like that because they have no understanding of good and evil. But I who have contemplated the essential beauty of good and the essential ugliness of evil, who know that the nature of the wrongdoer is of one kin with mine—not indeed of the same blood or seed but sharing the same mind, the same portion of the divine—I cannot be harmed by any one of them, and no one can involve me in shame. I cannot feel anger against him who is of my kin, nor hate

him. We were born to labor together, like the feet, the hands, the eyes, and the rows of upper and lower teeth. To work against one another is therefore contrary to nature, and to be angry against a man or turn one's back on him is to work against him. [33]

Citizens of the World   As all Stoics, Aurelius believed that people are not just citizens of a state or a nation but also citizens of the world. There is a kinship of all life, and all humans are brothers and sisters. The Stoics may have been the first school of philosophy to advance the notion of universal brotherhood. Unlike the Cynics, the Stoics considered that involvement in politics was often necessary to promote a kinder, gentler, more rational world.

If the power of thought is universal among mankind, so likewise is the possession of reason, making us rational creatures. It follows, therefore, that this reason speaks no less universally to us all with its "thou shalt" or "thou shalt not." So then there is a world-law, which in turn means that we are all fellow citizens and share a common citizenship and that the world is a single city. [34]

The Skeptic School

The word *skeptic* comes from the Greek *skeptikoi*, which means "doubter." The Sophists believed that, even if there were an absolute truth, we could not know it. The Skeptics agreed. They questioned the Stoic notion that we can know God or the way the universe operates. They also questioned Plato, Aristotle, and the Epicureans because they each held a different conception of truth. Like the Sophists, the Skeptics questioned any philosopher or philosophy that claimed to know the truth.

Skeptics did not deny the existence of truth, but they doubted that anyone had found it, or would ever find it.

Sextus Empiricus

A physician and philosopher, Sextus Empiricus (third century A.D.) thought that everything we experience has many explanations, and one explanation is as valid as the next. Thus, if we suspend judgment by not denying or affirming anything, we could live a balanced and calm life.

The Senses   Our five senses, said Sextus Empiricus, give us different impressions about the same object. For instance, imagine that you and a friend are walking down the street and you see two people coming toward you. "Look," you say to your friend, "here come John and Judy." As they get closer, however, you realize they are not John and Judy; they are Mike and Michelle. It is true that you had the sense impression, but the people looked different to you from a distance than they did up close. That is why Empiricus said we could never be certain that what we "see" with our senses is accurate. In the same way, we cannot be sure that our knowledge about the world or anything else is true or not true. That is why it is wise to suspend judgment.

Morality   According to Sextus Empiricus, moral ideas are as subject to doubt as trusting our senses. Cultures have different ideas about what is good and what is bad. Because we cannot know truth even if there is truth, one moral opinion is about as good as another according to Skepticism. For that reason, we should withhold moral judgment. If we take a stand on moral questions, our emotions flare. By suspending judgment, we remain serene and have peace of mind, claims Empiricus.

The man who opines that anything is by nature good or bad is forever being disquieted: when he is without the things which he deems good he believes himself to be tormented by things naturally bad and he pursues after the things which are, as he thinks, good; which when he has obtained he keeps falling into still more perturbations because of his irrational and immoderate elation, and in his dread of a change of fortune he uses every endeavour to avoid losing the things which he deems good. On the other hand, the man who determines nothing as to what is naturally good or bad neither shuns nor pursues anything eagerly; and, in consequence, he is unperturbed. [35]

The Neoplatonism School

We find the roots of Cynicism, Epicureanism, and Stoicism in both the pre-Socratic philosophers Heraclitus and Democritus and in the way Socrates lived and died. The Skeptic school of thought dates back to the Sophists. In the late Hellenistic period, Neoplatonism became the dominant philosophy. The founder of Neoplatonism was the great mystic Plotinus, who was inspired by Plato. Although Plotinus did not mention Christianity in his writings, his philosophy had a major influence on St. Augustine, one of the most famous Christian philosophers of the Middle Ages. Philosophers agree that Plotinus built the bridge between classical Greek philosophy and the medieval philosophers.

Plotinus

Plotinus (A.D. 204–270), a native of Lycopolis, Egypt, came to Alexandria when he was about 28 years old and studied under the philosopher Ammonius Saccas. When Plotinus was 39, he started his own school of philosophy in Rome that attracted many influential people, including the Emperor Gallenius. Plotinus was a popular lecturer with high spiritual ideals. One of his goals was to develop a city based on Plato's *Republic*, called "Platonopolis," but the city was never constructed.

Plotinus wrote 54 treatises, which he never put in particular order, and his weak eyesight prevented him from rereading them. After Plotinus died, his student Porphyry arranged the treatises into six sets of nine volumes called the *Enneads*. As a mystic, a person who experiences merging with God or the cosmic spirit, Plotinus realized a union with God six times in his life. Porphyry was with him four of those times. He wrote of his experience that, "[Plotinus's] end goal was to be united to, to approach the God who is over all things. Four times while I was with him, he attained that goal, in an unspeakable actuality and not in potency only." [36]

At age 64, almost blind and suffering ill health, Plotinus retired to a friend's estate where he died two years later.

God, or the One   Plotinus called God "the One." The One is the source of everything and the source that we must return. The One overflows eternally, and in doing so, forms the universe.

Plotinus looked to Plato and Aristotle for many of his ideas, but he objected to Aristotle's beliefs that the soul is the form of the body and cannot exist without a body. Like Plato, Plotinus thought the soul did not depend on the body for its existence. The universe, he said, is a living structure that goes on eternally from its source in the One. The One first overflows, or emanates, from itself to form nous, which is pure thought, or divine mind. Nous overflows into heavenly materials, forming the world soul. From the world soul, nous emanates various levels of activity to shape matter, or the physical world, and everything in it. Plotinus explained that humans could ascend upward toward the source by self-purification. The aim of the human soul, according to Plotinus, is to experience union with God, "which alone can satisfy it."

Emanation   Plotinus's theory of emanation is similar to the idea of water flowing from a spring that has no source outside itself. Plotinus also used the Sun as an analogy. The One emanates in the same way that light flows from the Sun. The Sun never exhausts itself; instead, it generates light rays that are not the Sun itself. In a similar manner, the One is the source of all things but is not all things.

Nous, or the divine mind, is universal intelligence and the rational order of the world. Nous contains the ideas or blueprints of all things, much like Plato's Forms. As nous overflows, it generates the world soul, which has two aspects. First, it looks

This sarcophagus, a stone container for a coffin or body, is from the late third century or early fourth century A.D. It is said to have contained the body of Plotinus (shown in center), the Father of Neoplatonism. Plotinus believed there is a supreme One, the source of everything, beyond all description of being and nonbeing.

upward to the divine mind and contemplates eternal ideas, and second, it emanates *downward*, generating the life-principle in all nature.

The human soul emanates from the world soul and also has two aspects. First, gazing up, it shares in the world soul and the divine mind. Second, looking down, the human soul connects with the physical body. Plotinus agreed with Plato that the human soul preexists in the world soul and is the result of a "fall" when it joins with the body. The soul gives the body life, the five senses, and reason.

When the physical body dies, the soul leaves the body and eventually takes birth again in another body. When the soul reaches the highest state of knowledge and love after many rebirths, it joins all other souls again in the world soul. Unlike Aristotle, Plotinus believed souls are immortal.

Ascent of the Soul   When the One descends into the lower realms, it shares as much of its perfection as possible with them. However, the process is not only of descent; it is a double movement of descent and ascent. Although the journey is a difficult and painful process that includes many lifetimes, all things ascend, seeking to reunite with their source. As we ascend, we develop moral values, the love of beauty, and disciplined thinking. The goal, for all humans, according to Plotinus, is to attain likeness to God by "becoming just and holy, and living by wisdom," through ascent. In his treatise on beauty, Plotinus described the way of the soul's return:

> Withdraw into yourself, and look. And if you do not find yourself beautiful yet, act as does the creator of a statue that is to be made beautiful. He cuts away here, he smoothes there, he makes this line lighter, this other purer, until a lovely face has grown upon his work. So

do you also: cut away all that is excessive, straighten all that is crooked, bring light to all that is overcast, labour to make all one glow of beauty and never cease chiseling your statue, until there shall shine out on you from it the godlike splendour of virtue, until you shall see the perfect goodness surely established in the stainless shrine.

When you know that you have become this perfect work . . . when you find yourself wholly true to your essential nature . . . you are now become very vision; now call up all your confidence, strike forward yet a step— you need a guide no longer–strain, and see. [37]

The philosophy of Plotinus, especially his idea of liberating the soul to a mystical union with God, strongly influenced Christian mystics in the Catholic Church and was the source and inspiration for most Western mystics in the years to come.

Hypatia of Alexandria

Hypatia (c. A.D. 370–415), a woman of Egyptian and Greek descent, was a philosopher, mathematician, and astronomer. She was appointed to the position of philosopher at the museum of Alexandria, Egypt. The appointment was an unusual type of honor for a woman. She brilliantly taught the philosophies of Plato, Aristotle, and Neoplatonism. Like Plotinus, she believed in a divine source, the One. Like Plotinus, her goal was to unite with the One, and she shared her methods with a select circle of students, teaching them to seek the divine part of human nature, or the soul. She called it, "the eye buried within us."

Many intellects considered Hypatia the greatest philosopher of her day, and the Roman governor often asked her advice on city affairs. However, as a pagan woman in a Christian world, she paid for her talents with her life. One day, a group of

Christian monks pulled her out of her chariot, ripped off her clothes, and cut her body to pieces with sharp shells until she died. Then, they mutilated her body and burned it to ashes.

SUMMARY AND LINKS TO THE MEDIEVAL WORLD

The first philosophers in the Western world, known as pre-Socratics, were Thales, Anaxamander, Anaximenes, Pythagoras, Heraclitus, Parmenides, Zeno, Empedocles, Anaxagoras, and the atomists. Each philosopher probed the nature of the universe by moving away from religious mythology to scientific investigation. They discovered the importance of change and permanence, numbers and atoms.

Next to arrive on the philosophical scene were the Sophists, Protagoras, Gorgias, and Thrasymachus. As Sophists, they thought that, even if there were ultimate truths, the human mind is not capable of knowing them. For them, knowledge is limited to the situation at hand.

Socrates did not agree with the Sophists that we could not know ultimate truth. He thought that knowledge of ultimate truth is possible and it is the highest good. We can gain knowledge of the truth by caring for the soul and through self-examination. For him, without such knowledge, moral virtue is impossible. Only by attaining knowledge of the Good can we be happy.

Plato agreed with Socrates that we can know the soul and the eternal Forms: Truth, Beauty, and Goodness. He explained how we can achieve this goal in his "Allegory of the Cave" and "The Divided Line." We can also achieve knowledge through love as described in the *Symposium*. In his ideal state, Plato said the highest part of the soul (reason/intuition) must rule.

With the coming of Christianity, we find a rejection of the naturalistic ideas of the Hellenistic philosophers in favor of a personal and transcendent God. Christians would not accept the Stoic view that "God is in all and all is in God," nor would they accept the Cynic, Epicurean, and Skeptic view of God, the world, or the afterlife. Christians looked to separate God from science, so that they could concentrate on God alone. The philosophies that grew from the medieval Christian thinkers would have a profound impact throughout the world that lasts to this day.

NOTES

CHAPTER 1

1. Hesiod, *Works and Days, in Hesiod: The Homeric Hymns and Homerica,* trans. by H.G. Eyelyn-White. Cambridge: Harvard University Press, 1926, pp. 3, 9, 19.
2. John Burnet, *Early Greek Philosophy*, 4th ed. New York: World Publishing, 1967, pp.70–71.
3. Ibid., p 73.
4. Ibid., p. 96.
5. Holger Thesleff, "Pythagorean Texts of the Hellenistic Period, 'Acta Academiae Aboensis—Humaniora,'" in *A History of Women Philosophers*, ed. by Mary Ellen Waithe, trans. by Vicki Lynn Harper. Vol. 1, 600 B.V.–500 A.S. Dordrecht, Netherlands: Martinus Nijhoff Publishers, 1987, p. 32.
6. Burnet, p. 134.
7. W.T. Jones, *The Classical Mind: A History of Ancient Philosophy*. New York: Harcourt Brace Jovanovich, 1970, p. 22.
8. Burnet, p. 318.
9. Ibid.
10. Ibid., pp. 207–208.
11. Ibid., p. 260.
12. Diogenes Laertius, *Lives and Opinions of Eminent Philosophers*, trans. by R.D. Hicks. Vol. 11. Cambridge: Loeb Classical Library, Harvard University Press, 1925, p. 453.
13. *Source Book in Ancient Philosophy*, trans. by C.M. Bakewell. New York: Scribner, 1907, pp. 63–64.

CHAPTER 2

14. Plato, "Theaetetus," in *Plato: The Collected Dialogues*, ed. by Edith Hamilton and Huntington Cairns, trans. by F.M. Cornford. New York: Random House, 1966, pp. 856–857.
15. Plato, "Gorgias," in *Plato: The Collected Dialogues*, Sections 452e and 456b, ed. by Edith Hamilton and Huntington Cairns, trans. by W.D. Woodhead. New York: Random House, 1966, pp. 236, 237.
16. Plato, *The Republic of Plato*, trans. by F.M Cornford. London: Oxford University Press, 1974, p. 26.
17. Karl Jaspers, "Socrates, Confucius, Buddha, Jesus," in *The Great Philosophers*. Vol. I. New York: Harcourt, Brace & World, 1962, p. 6.
18. Plato, "Euthyphro," in *Euthyphro, Apology, Crito*, trans. byF.J. Church. New York: Bobbs-Merrill, 1956, pp. 12, 13.
19. Plato, "Apology," XVIII, 31 in *Euthyphro, Apology, Crito*, p. 37.
20. Ibid., XXVI, 36, p. 44.
21. Plato, "Phaedo," in *Plato: The Collected Dialogues*, ed. by Edith Hamilton and Huntington Cairns, trans. by Hugh Tredennick. New York: Bollingen Foundation, Random House, 1966, p. 98.

CHAPTER 3

22. Plato, "Phaedo," in *Philosophic Classics*. Vol. I: *Ancient Philosophy*, 2nd ed, Sections 106d

and 106e, ed. by F.E. Baird and Walter Kaufman, trans. by F.J. Church. New Jersey: Prentice Hall, 1994, p. 106.

23. Plato, *The Republic*, trans. by H.D.P. Lee. Baltimore: Penguin Books, 1967, pp. 276–277, 510–511.

24. Ibid., pp. 278, 511.

25. Plato, "The Symposium," 210c–212c, in *The Collected Dialogues of Plato*, ed. by Edith Hamilton and Huntington Cairns, trans. by Michael Joyce. New York: Random House, 1963, copyright 1989 by Princeton University Press, pp. 556–563.

CHAPTER 4

26. Aristotle, "Metaphysica," Bk. 12.6, 1072A, and 12.7, 1072b, 15, in *The Basic Works of Aristotle*, ed. by Richard McKeon, trans. by W.D. Ross. New York: Random House, 1941, pp. 878–879.

27. Aristotle, "De Anima," in *The Basic Works*, Bk. II, Ch. 1, 412a 5–15, ed. by Richard McKeon, trans. by J.A. Smith. New York: Random House, 1941, pp. 554–555.

28. Ibid., Bk. III, Ch. 4. 3. 429b–430, p. 591.

29. Aristotle, "The Nichomachean Ethics," in *The Basic Works*, Bk. 1, 1094a, ed. by Richard

McKeon, trans. by W.D. Ross. New York: Random House, 1941, p. 935.

30. Ibid., Bk..1, 1097 a & b, pp. 941–942.

CHAPTER 5

31. Epicurus, "Letter to Menoeceus," in *Epicurus: The Extant Remains*, trans. by C. Bailey. Oxford: New Oxford University Press, 1926, 127 ff., p. 87.

32. Epictetus, *Encheiridion*, trans. by W.A. Oldfather. Cambridge: Harvard University Press, 1928, Sections 1, 8.

33. Marcus Aurelius, *The Meditations*, trans. by G.M.A. Grube. New York: Library of Liberal Arts, 1963, Bk. II, 1a, p. 11.

34. Marcus Aurelius, *The Meditations*, trans. by Maxwell Staniforth. New York: Penguin Books, 1964, 6. 41.

35. Sextus Empiricus, *Outlines of Pyrrhonism*, trans. by R.G. Bury. Vol I. Cambridge: Harvard University Press, 1933, Bk. 1, pp. 26–27.

36. Porphyry, "The Life of Plotinus," in *Plotinus*, trans. by A.H. Armstrong. Vol. I. Cambridge: Harvard University Press, 1966, p. 71.

37. Plotinus, *The Enneads*, trans. by Stephen MacKenna. London: Faber & Faber, 1917–1930, Book I, 6. 9.

GLOSSARY

allegory The expression by means of fictional figures and actions of truths or generalizations about human existence.

appearance The way things present themselves to our five senses in contrast to their true reality.

aristocracy A government or state ruled by an elite or privileged upper class.

Being A general term in metaphysics referring to ultimate reality.

cause That which has the power to produce a change in another thing.

city-state An autonomous state consisting of a city and surrounding territory.

cynic An individual who lives an austere, unconventional life based on Cynic doctrine.

dialectic method A question-and-answer technique used by Socrates that leads one from mere opinion to knowledge.

dialogue A written composition in which two or more characters are conversing.

element One of a class of substances such as earth, air, fire, and water.

emanate To flow out of or overflow.

Epicurean The school of philosophy that believed pleasure is the highest good.

essence The main characteristic or quality that makes a thing uniquely itself.

ethics The field of philosophy that studies value judgments of good and evil, right and wrong.

fallacy A misleading or false argument; an unsound reasoning.

Forms   In Plato's view, Forms are the ideal patterns beyond space/time. Forms are the true reality, immaterial,
and eternal.

hedonism   The pursuit of pleasure.

holistic   Relating to wholes or complete systems rather than
a dissection of their parts.

illusion   A false or misleading impression of reality.

immoral   Morally wrong; bad or not right.

immortality   Everlasting soul or spirit.

indivisible   Not separated into parts.

logic   The laws of reason; thinking correctly.

macrocosm   The universe as a whole.

materialism   The belief that everything is composed of matter and can be explained by physical laws.

mean   For Aristotle, a mean is the midpoint between
two extremes.

metaphysics   The field of philosophy concerned with the
ultimate nature of reality; speculation of things beyond the
physical world.

meteorology   The science that deals with the atmosphere,
weather, and climate.

microcosm   A miniature world or individual as compared to
the macrocosm.

monism   The view that everything consists of only one ultimate substance such as matter or spirit.

mystic   One who experiences an intimate union of the soul
with God; one who understands the mysteries of life.

natural philosopher   One who believes that matter is the
ultimate substance.

nous   The Greek word for mind or intelligence.

oracle   A shrine in which a god reveals hidden knowledge;
the person through whom the god is believed to speak.

pantheism   The view that God is in the world and the world is in God.

paradox   A seemingly contradictory statement that expresses a possible truth.

philosopher   A term first coined by Pythagoras meaning "lover of wisdom."

philosophy   The rational investigation of the truths and principles in ethics, metaphysics, logic, knowledge, and other related fields.

quantitative mathematician   A mathematician who measures everything by amount or quantity.

reincarnation   The passing of the immortal soul through many cycles of birth, death, and rebirth.

relativism   The view that there is no absolute knowledge and that truth is different for each individual and society.

simile   A figure of speech in which two different things are compared to one another.

skeptic   A person who questions our ability to have knowledge of reality.

Sophists   Teachers in ancient Greece who taught rhetoric to young men preparing for the law or political careers.

Stoicism   The school of philosophy that views self-control and acceptance of one's fate as important factors in gaining happiness.

substance   That which exists in its own right and depends on nothing else; the essence of all things.

universal Logos   The rational ordering principle of the world, according to Heraclitus and the Stoics.

utopia   A perfect or ideal society.

virtue   A morally excellent quality of character.

BIBLIOGRAPHY

Aristotle. "De Anima," in *The Basic Works of Aristotle*, Vol. III, ed. by Richard McKeon, trans. by J.A. Smith. New York: Random House, 1941.

———. "Metaphysica," in *The Basic Works of Aristotle*, ed. by Richard McKeon, trans. by W.D.Ross. New York: Random House, 1941.

———. "The Nichomachean Ethics," in *The Basic Works of Aristotle*, ed. by Richard McKeon, trans. by W.D. Ross. New York: Random House, 1941.

Aurelius, Marcus. *The Meditations*, trans. by Maxwell Staniforth. New York: Penguin Books, 1964.

———. *The Meditations*, trans. by G.M.A. Grube. New York: Library of Liberal Arts, 1963.

Burnet, John. *Early Greek Philosophy*, 4th ed. New York: World Publishing, 1967.

Empiricus, Sextus. *Outlines of Pyrrhonism*, Vol I, trans. by R.G. Bury. Cambridge: Harvard University Press, 1933.

Epictetus. *Encheiridion*, trans. by W.A. Oldfather. Cambridge: Harvard University Press, 1928.

Epicurus. "Letter to Menoeceus," in *Epicurus: The Extant Remains*, trans. by C. Bailey. Oxford: New Oxford University Press, 1926.

Hesiod. *Works and Days, in Hesiod: The Homeric Hymns and Homerica*, trans. by H.G. Eyelyn-White. Cambridge: Harvard University Press, 1926.

Jaspers, Karl. "Socrates, Confucius, Buddha, Jesus," in *The Great Philosophers*, Vol. I. New York: Harcourt, Brace & World, 1962.

Jones, W.T. *The Classical Mind: A History of Ancient Philosophy*. New York: Harcourt Brace Jovanovich Publishers, 1970.

Laertius, Diogenes. *Lives and Opinions of Eminent Philosophers*, Vol. 11, trans. by R.D. Hicks. Cambridge: Loeb Classical Library, Harvard University Press, 1925.

Plato. "Apology," XVIII. 31, in *Euthyphro, Apology, Crito*, trans. by F.J. Church. New York: Bobbs-Merrill, 1956.

———. "Euthyphro," in *Euthyphro, Apology, Crito*, trans. by F.J. Church. New York: Bobbs-Merrill, 1956.

————. "Gorgias," in *Plato: The Collected Dialogues*, ed. by Edith Hamilton and Huntington Cairns, trans. by W.D. Woodhead. New York: Random House, 1966.

————. "Phaedo," in *Plato: The Collected Dialogues*, ed. by Edith Hamilton and Huntington Cairns, trans. by Hugh Tredennick. New York: Bollingen Foundation, Random House, 1966.

————. "Phaedo," in *Philosophic Classics*, Vol. I: *Ancient Philosophy, 2nd ed.*, ed. by F.E. Baird and Walter Kaufman, trans. by F.J. Church. New Jersey: Prentice Hall, 1994.

————. *The Republic*, trans. by H.D.P. Lee. Baltimore: Penguin Books, 1967.

————. *The Republic of Plato*, trans. by F.M Cornford. London: Oxford University Press, 1974.

————. "The Symposium," in *The Collected Dialogues of Plato*, ed. by Edith Hamilton and Huntington Cairns, trans. by Michael Joyce. New York: Random House, 1963, copyright 1989 by Princeton University Press.

————. "Theaetetus," in *Plato: The Collected Dialogues*, ed. by Edith Hamilton and Huntington Cairns, trans. by F.M. Cornford. New York: Random House, 1966.

Plotinus. *The Enneads*, trans. by Stephen Mac Kenna. London: Faber & Faber, 1917–1930.

Porphyry. "The Life of Plotinus," Vol. I, in *Plotinus*, trans. by A.H. Armstrong. Cambridge: Harvard University Press, 1966.

Source Book in Ancient Philosophy, trans. by C.M. Bakewell. New York: Scribner, 1907.

Thesleff, Holger. "Pythagorean Texts of the Hellenistic Period, 'Acta Academiae Aboensis—Humaniora' " in *A History of Women Philosophers*, Vol. 1, 600 B.V.–500 A.S., ed. by Mary Ellen Waithe, trans. by Vicki Lynn Harper. Dordrecht, Netherlands: Martinus Nijhoff Publishers, 1987.

FURTHER READING

BOOKS

Branham, R. Bracht, and Marie-Odile Goulet-Cazé, eds. *The Cynics: The Cynic Movement in Antiquity and Its Legacy*. Berkeley: University of California Press, 2000.

Cooper, Sharon Katz. *Aristotle: Philosopher, Teacher, and Scientist*. Mankato, Minn: Compass Point Books, 2006.

Curd, Patricia. *The Legacy of Parmenides: Eleatic Monism and Later Presocratic Thought*. Las Vegas: Parmenides Publishing, 2004.

Guthrie, W.K.C. *Socrates*. Cambridge: Cambridge University Press, 2003.

Long, A.A. *Epictetus: A Stoic and Socratic Guide to Life*. New York: Oxford University Press, 2004.

Magee, Bryan. *The Great Philosophers: An Introduction to Western Philosophy*. New York: Oxford University Press, 2000.

Taylor, A.E. *Plato: The Man and His Work*. Mineola, NY: Dover Publications, 2001.

Taylor, C.C.W., trans. *The Atomists: Leucippus and Democritus: Fragments*. Toronto: University of Toronto Press, 1999.

WEB SITES

Andrew Irvine's lecture on Hellenistic Philosophy (Sep. 24, 1998)

http://people.bu.edu/wwildman/WeirdWildWeb/courses/wphil/lectures/wphil_theme04.htm

The Big View's Information on Greek Philosophy

www.thebigview.com/greeks/

Dictionary of Philosophical Terms and Names

www.philosophypages.com/dy/

Drury University's Information on the Pre-Socratic Philosophers

www.drury.edu/ess/History/Ancient/PreSocOV.html

The Internet Encyclopedia of Philosophy

http://www.iep.utm.edu/

John Burnet's *Early Greek Philosophy*

http://faculty.evansville.edu/tb2/courses/phil211/burnet/

Radical Academy's Page on the Sophists

www.radicalacademy.com/philsophists.htm

University of Florida Ancient Philosophy Page

web.uflib.ufl.edu/cm/classics/Ancient%20Philosophy.htm

PICTURE CREDITS

INDEX

ABOUT THE AUTHOR

JOAN A. PRICE has a Ph.D. in philosophy from Arizona State University. She was a philosophy professor at Mesa Community College for 30 years and cofounder of the Department of Religious Studies. She was chairperson of the Department of Philosophy and Religious Studies for five years and at present is professor emeritus of philosophy at Mesa Community College.

Price has written dozens of magazine and journal articles and is the author of *Truth is a Bright Star: A Hopi Adventure,* translated into Japanese and Korean; *Hawk in the Wind; Medicine Man; J.K. Rowling: A Biography; Understanding Philosophy;* and *Great Religious Leaders* for middle-grade and young adult readers. Her adult books include *Introduction to Sri Aurobindo's Philosophy; Philosophy Through the Ages,* a textbook for college students; and *Climbing the Spiritual Ladder.*

She is an animal lover with three dogs and several flocks of wild geese and ducks that camp on the lake by her house for daily handouts. She lives in Scottsdale, Arizona.